"He is a Bum - only in name. One of the most generous, loyal, and caring individuals I have ever known in sport. He balanced leadership and friendship better than anyone who ever stood on an NFL sideline. We can all learn from him and his remarkable life."

Jim Nantz,
Emmy Award-winning CBS Sports broadcaster

"People go through life never having the chance to experience special times and special people. I was lucky to have had the opportunity to share all of this with Bum Phillips and I feel blessed having done so. It is an honor to have shared my life with him."

Dan Pastorini,
Former quarterback of the Houston Oilers

"Bum Phillips' book … will be a blessing to you. He was a great football coach as well as a mentor to hundreds of football players. To me, his greatest accomplishment is the fact that he found the Lord Jesus as his Saviour at age 76. God helped him to succeed in his career because His gracious Hand was upon him. I love you, Debbie and Bum, and I salute you!"

Dodie Osteen,
Co-Founder of Houston's Lakewood Church

"When you read this book, it's like being on the sideline with Bum Phillips, who coaches you up as only he can do. I love my coach and you will, too."

Mike Barber,
Pro Claim founder and former tight end for the Houston Oilers

"This book blew me away! I am the No. 1 fan of Luv ya Blue and Bum Phillips, and I'm still floored with the Bum I never knew: Marine Hero, Coach, Southern Gentleman, Family Man! Add to the list: Born Again. And it shows. WOW DOES IT SHOW! It will leave you in awe of the real Coach Phillips. Three words sum up the impact and scope of this book: The Lord, The Love, The Legacy. It's much, much more than just one great read."

Dr. John Bisagno,
Paster F

Bum Phillips: Coach, Cowboy, Christian

Copyright © 2010 by Bum Phillips

Published by Lucid Books in Brenham, TX.
www.LucidBooks.net

First Printing 2010

All Scripture quotations are from
New International Version Published by Tyndale House Publishers, Inc. of Wheaton, Illinois and Zonderman Publishing House of Grand Rapids, Michigan.

ISBN-13: 9781935909026

BUM PHILLIPS

COACH · COWBOY · CHRISTIAN

AN **AUTOBIOGRAPHY** BY
BUM PHILLIPS

WITH
GABE SEMENZA

A WORD FROM BUM

As with any endeavor of this sort, many details have to be left out. The agents tell us folks don't read long books these days, so keep it as short as possible and to the point. The original point of this book was to leave a chronicle of my life for my children, grandchildren and great grandchildren.

I have often wished my grandfathers kept journals or that I had the foresight to pump them for information about their lives before they ever thought of having children, much less grandchildren. I wished I had information about my dad's father's times when he worked on the JA Ranch and trailed cattle all the way to Kansas. I wish my mother's father kept a journal about his early years, too.

So with Debbie's prodding, I set about to put this book together with the help of Gabe Semenza, family and friends. As you might imagine when you start something like this at age 86, some of your memories are a little fuzzy, but then there aren't many of my contemporaries out there to correct anything.

Anyway, I am writing this to say to all of my dear family and friends: If your name does not appear in print, it in no way has any bearing on how I feel about you. You know that I love each and every one of you, that I cherish the parts you have played in my life and that I fondly think of you often. But here's the deal: This book is a chronicle of my life as told to and talked about with Gabe Semenza. Because we spent many hours together, Gabe was a recent addition to our "family." We put these memoirs together for me from input from whomever he could get to respond, as well as my own recollections.

The amount of ink any particular family member or friend gets is directly related to how much time, effort and input they put into the writing of this book. It doesn't mean I love them more than those who were unable to devote more time to this project. It just means they made themselves available to help bring this about. Please know I love all my kids the same.

BUM PHILLIPS

FOREWORD

Even in my best moment, I would fall way short of expressing my love and respect for my coach, Bum Phillips! He's more than just a coach to me. He is more like the father I never had. I have always said: "Bum has five daughters and one son, but many kids, and I am so blessed to be one of his kids."

Everything I have – including my family and our prison ministry – I owe to God and my coach. Coach was always more interested in me and my life than just my NFL career or what I could do for the Houston Oilers.

It doesn't matter whether you love sports or not, all of us come to a place and time when the clock is running out, it's the fourth quarter and we find ourselves about to make the biggest call of our life. That's when we find we need a coach. In two minutes Coach Bum Phillips can say more than most can say in two hours. Because of who he is there is no audience he cannot coach!

I've witnessed Coach Phillips gather the roughest of inmates all around him inside of prison. When he's done with them, they ask: "What must I do to be saved?" Today, Coach is focused on the real game: The Game of Life.

His down-to-Earth honesty, humility and integrity stayed with him from Orange, Texas, to the sidelines of the NFL and now to each and every one of you. When you read this book, it's like being on the sideline with Bum Phillips, who coaches you up as only he can do. I love my coach and you will, too.

Mike Barber
Pro Claim founder and
former tight end for the Houston Oilers

PREFACE

I magine, if you will, leaning against the back of a stiff wooden chair. You sit straight. A dormant, stone fireplace to your right looms quietly like a blackened cavern. The afternoon aroma of sweetened tea and fresh chicken salad drift by, carried by the heat of a summer indoors. You're in South Texas, surrounded by bronze cowboy sculptures and paintings, nestled into a casual living room.

Bum Phillips rests four feet in front of you on his oversized leather chair. He stares out the window to his right. The view frames the back end of his 250-acre Goliad, Texas, ranch. For a moment, he seems lost in the brush-cleared fields of August.

You turn your gaze to the spurs on the mantle and think at once of the horses outside. The animals, beautiful and proud, display a brand befitting a horse here: a football wrapped inside a cowboy hat.

Bum, 86 now, discusses John Wayne movies, the battles he survived during World War II and the football legends he will forever remain linked to: Paul "Bear" Bryant, Earl Campbell, Terry Bradshaw.

The soil where Bum lives is not unlike the ground he traveled as a boy, although his home dwarfs the wooden shanty of his childhood. Dusty journeys by wagon, the table scraps of the Great Depression, are now distant memories.

Bum remains widely famous for his down-home Texas yarns, for wearing a cowboy hat and boots during a time when fedoras and dress shoes graced pro football sidelines. These iconic memories pale, however, against the much richer story that emerges at second glance.

You examine the room again. You lean forward and twist your body to scan the wall behind you. No National Football League memorabilia. No Houston Oilers jerseys. No photographs of Bum prowling pro football sidelines. The family donated much of its most valuable treasures – at least those that garner large sums at celebrity auctions – to charity. This decorative omission begins to unravel a story that starts long ago on the E.W. Brown Estate – hundreds of miles to the east and north.

On a bookshelf by the fireplace, a title stands out: "God's Coach." To those who knew Bum early in his career, the book would seem out of place, an anomaly. Bum lived his entire football career and much of his life devoid of scripture and prayer. He believed if he lived his life properly, treated others well and kept his word, he'd go to heaven. That changed the year the famed coach turned 76.

Now, friends and family say God acted in his life all along. God pulled him in this direction and that, propelled him to the limelight and to places later in life where his good name served even greater purposes.

How did a rough and tough, oft-criticized but beloved football coach and cowboy end up spreading the gospel to inmates? What compels this 86-year-old legend to rise from his comfortable leather chair to spend time in maximum-security prisons?

Imagine now that you rise from the stiff wooden chair. You step toward the nearby sofa, sit and lean against the thick rust-brown cushions. Bum shifts his stare from the window, fixes those kind eyes on you and says he's ready to tell all. This is his story.

CHAPTER 1

THE HARD WAY

*"Train a child in the way he should go, and when he is
old he will not turn from it." – Proverbs 22:6*

I've always said people think far more of me than I ever
did of myself. Admiration just came with the turf. So
why write a book? I suppose I have some stories to tell.
You can't play and coach football for 50 years without gaining
valuable lessons. You can't live 86 years without learning what
works, what doesn't.

My name is Bum Phillips. Remember: Bum is a nickname,
not a description. If you know me by my nickname, you likely
remember my days on pro football sidelines. I was the coach
with the cowboy hat, boots and plug of Tinsley, which I've
chewed on since 1937.

It's funny how things work out for a guy. The greatest
lesson I learned in life presented itself away from football
and while I chewed on a thoughtful question from a friend.
If you learn nothing else from this book than the importance
of that lesson, I've done my job here. We'll get to that story
a bit later.

I want first to explain a few things: Where I come from,
why I still wear cowboy hats and what happened behind the

scenes of my favorite National Football League times. Football did more for me than I ever did for it, and I hope this book offers people as much value as the sport offered to me and my family.

Christianity became a big part of my life – and thus a big part of my story – even if I steered away from it until I was 76 years old. I'm not the type of guy, though, who wants to shove anything down anyone's throat. I'll simply share my Christian story and hope you learn from my mistakes. You don't want regrets at my age – when there is no time left in the game.

Now, let's turn back the clock. I've got quite a bit to say about my childhood.

People in East Texas are sticklers for claiming their rightful birthplaces, and I'm no different. Many people have written I was born in Beaumont. Now, I have nothing against Beaumont, but I was born in Orange, Texas. On my 84th birthday, John Dubose, an Orange County commissioner, proclaimed I was one of Orange County's brightest stars (1). Townspeople refer to the day as "Bum Phillips Day." I'm not sure what they do on that day, but the gesture reminds me of how grateful I am I was born there.

Orange was born in 1836 – 87 years before I showed up – and the year Texas won its independence from Mexico (2). Native orange groves attracted the hungry boatmen who navigated the Sabine River. You'd think I'd love oranges. I don't. Every spring, my Mama insisted I swallow castor oil, a pale yellow liquid extracted from castor seed. She figured it cleansed the body, purified me. The catch: It tasted like hell and I hated it. To ensure I'd guzzle the stuff once a year, Mama dripped the liquid into my orange juice, which I can't drink to this day. My wife eats oranges as part of her diet, but I don't even like to look at the peels.

Orange is the state's easternmost city. A strong-armed quarterback could heave a rock from the Texas side of the Sabine River and make a splash in Louisiana's marshy western edge. You can't see the Gulf of Mexico from Orange, but it's close, too. You understand now why I still love a hot bowl of Capt. Benny's seafood gumbo.

In Orange's early days, the city became a pass-through for outlaws and renegades. Louisiana outlaws fled their state for Texas; Texas Rangers chased homegrown outlaws east and across the Sabine. I would have loved to watch the Rangers chase those bad boys, but I'm glad I wasn't there to see those who were caught by vigilantes. My hometown, more than a century ago, planted what matured into a famous hanging tree.

By the late 1800s, Orange blossomed with almost 20 steam sawmills (3). Despite its location on the state's outer extreme, my city became the center of the Texas lumber industry. Later, large machines dredged the Port of Orange, and thick-handed men went to work building ships, many of which floated on trees milled from nearby. When World War I ended in 1918, demand for the town's bread and butter exports decreased, and the deepwater port turned into a hotspot for speakeasies, gamblers and bootleggers.

By the time I was born, Orange was a strategic link between Louisiana and Texas. I don't remember this, of course, but I love history. I can imagine those old ships filled with cotton, lumber and cattle sailing the Sabine and Neches rivers. I remember stories about the businessmen who cashed in during the good times and who weathered the downtimes. They built elaborate mansions and paid men to manage their ranches.

E. W. Brown was no exception. Brown was an entrepreneur. He owned a home in Orange and a sprawling estate just outside town. As president of Orange's Yellow Pine Paper Mill and other companies, he became one of the wealthiest U.S. manufacturers (4). He also gave my maternal grandfather the job of managing his favorite ranch.

James Monroe Parish, my grandfather, managed the E. W. Brown Estate, the oldest cattle range in Orange, for almost 50 years. My Mama grew up there. They had horses and cattle. My grandfather struck a deal with Brown that afforded him a decent lifestyle. He managed Brown's ranch, and in exchange, he received half the cattle. This ranch served as my first glimpse into what became a lifelong passion.

Despite my hometown's citrus namesake, in some cowboy circles Orange is considered the first cattle-raising area in Texas. I always looked up to cowboys: hard-working cattlemen and horsemen. Even today, I hang a photograph of John Wayne near my front door. Nearby: 10 of my white cowboy hats, each resting snugly on a hook.

I'm not sure if critics thought I was crazy for wearing a cowboy hat and boots to NFL games, or if they figured I was just a dumb hick. I don't mind people thinking I'm stupid, but I don't want to give them any proof. I guess I always believed in being true to who you are. I was a cowboy long before I became a football coach.

I was born Oail Andrew Phillips on Sept. 29, 1923, three years after the formation of the American Professional Football Association. I don't remember most of the first couple years, but I'm told I was born in a house. Childbirth in those days often occurred outside hospitals. My first memory is of my older sister, Edrina, who hit me with a metal hoe. Evidently, I aggravated her. I don't know what I could have said at 3 years old to prompt an attack with a garden tool.

Gardening was a big part of our lives. We largely lived off the land. Mama served vegetables and fruit, which grow easily in this climate, with most meals. Because we lived without a

car and in a home eight miles outside Orange, trips to town
took hours. Luckily, we lived near my grandfather on the E.W.
Brown Estate, and his cattle provided our meat. We cooped
chickens for their eggs and drumsticks.

If we went to town, which was rare, we ventured by wagon
to load up with flour, sugar and lard. I'd sit up front with my
mother, Naomi, and beg for the chance to steer. She told me I
was too young, that a wrong turn could tip the rickety wagon
and send both of us flying into the rutted dirt road below. Even
at an early age, I yearned to hold the reigns. I was born with
a coach's instinct.

During those rare, humid trips to the Orange Grocery
Company, we passed the Southern Pacific Railroad Depot,
which delivered out-of-towners who clamored to popular
speakeasies. If it had rained recently, travel along the low-lying
roads became difficult at best. I wasn't worried about getting
stuck, though, with Mama on the wagon.

As I rode with my mother at the front of the wagon, I
watched the sawmills, tugboats and oxen moving logs. From
beneath my first cowboy hat, which my grandfather had
stuffed with tissue so that it clung to my boy-sized head, I
absorbed the ways of early Texans. By the time I was famous
I bought 20 cowboy hats a year and donated each to charity.
For years, I wore felt hats during the wintertime and straw hats
during summers. I never did wear the hat in domed stadiums,
though. Mama always told me not to wear a hat indoors.
Besides, you need a hat to keep the sun out of your eyes and
the rain off your head. It ain't raining inside, and there's no
sun in there either.

Because we rarely traveled to town, I received much of
my education on the ranch. I also grew up near eight aunts
and uncles, and all those cousins. I was kin to most everyone
I knew. We worked together and, for fun, we'd gather for
a Sunday fish fry near the river. During those gatherings, I

played with my cousins, the men played dominoes and the women cleaned the fish. It probably didn't cost five bucks to feed 25 people.

We were poor, but we didn't know any better. At 5 or 6 years old, I received a toy car from my aunt for Christmas. The push car was my only present but I was tickled to death. I didn't starve, and I didn't do without. It's just when blue jeans got holes in them, we patched them. Nowadays, you pay for jeans to come with the holes already in them.

Growing up, I didn't know what football was. We didn't even have running water let alone electricity. I couldn't have listened to football broadcasts or watched TV games if I'd wanted to. I knew cattle. Like most boys, I figured I'd work forever on a ranch, at a shipyard or in the oil fields. Work began for me at an early age.

When household chores were complete, my Mama loaded me into the wagon and we visited her father's ranch. She loved her father about as much as she loved horses. As a young boy I roped, pitched hay, worked the fields and helped to move my grandfather's livestock. I did everything from picking cotton to bending stocks on 80 acres of corn.

At the end of a long day, I'd climb back onto the wagon, kick the dust off my boots and make sure the beef grandfather packaged didn't bounce from the wooden seat and to the ground. The flat scenery rolled slowly by, and images of digging my small boots into a horse at full gallop filled my mind. I still remember those boots. As a grown man, I bought boots made from lizards and alligators. I wore kangaroo and ostrich boots, which I liked because they stretched to fit my feet.

We moved temporarily from the country and into Orange so I could attend Anderson School. The building was a three-story home renovated to educate elementary school children. It had a dome on top, a round porch for an entrance and dozens of windows. Inside, I was a raucous and noisy child. I received countless whippings for being too loud or argumentative. I had opinions and I never minded voicing them. One time, I told a teacher, "Oh, rats," and she sent me down the hallway. The principal whipped me on my back with a razor belt.

After a short stint in town, we returned to the country – and my sister Edrina and I took to fighting. She was beautiful, a future class valedictorian and full of personality. Like all people in my family, she was good at taking up for what she believed in. When we didn't fight, we used the headboard and footboard of Mama's and Daddy's bed for our pretend horses.

Edrina, it turns out, is also the one who gave me my famous nickname. Because of her stuttering, she couldn't say the word "brother." Her attempts came out "Bu-bu-bu-Bum." The name just stuck.

Jo Annette, my younger sister, wasn't born until I was 12. She offers a different version of the story.

"This will fly in the face of everything that has been said about where Bum got his name, but this is the true story," Jo Annette said. "Mama and Daddy went on a lot of picnics. Didn't have much money for anything else when Bum and Edrina were little. So, on this particular picnic, Bum was just crawling and made his way over to an old cow skull that was full of bumblebees. They of course stung him and after that, Mama started calling him Bumble. That's where Edrina got the name from because she couldn't say 'Bumble' and shortened it to 'Bum.'"

I'll let you decide which story to believe. I suppose I could have crawled through the grass headlong and into a beehive. I tell you what, though, something happened to me at an early age that created a resentment toward grass – at least the grooming part. For a reason I still can't explain, I hated to mow the lawn. Something about pushing a rusted, metal, hand-powered mower made my skin crawl. I'd get whippings for how I mowed. I wasn't lazy. I worked 14-hour days. But when I mowed the yard, I cut corners. I'd miss spots on purpose.

It might be no coincidence my first NFL head coaching job was with the Houston Oilers. Ten years earlier, the team unveiled the Astrodome, the world's first indoor baseball and football stadium. By the time I became head coach, engineers installed AstroTurf, thus removing the need for those doggone lawnmowers.

Like any kid, I grew up to be a mix of my Mama and my Daddy. I was closer, however, to my Mama. Daddy never did sit around the house, so I didn't get much of a chance to talk to him.

Mama was a stern woman, but she knew how to show love without ever saying it. She played harmonica and the guitar, and fostered my passion for music. To this day, I'm friends with musicians you know by name. Every now and again we invite a bunch out to stay on my Goliad, Texas, ranch. We spend weeks catching up, eating my wife's home cooking and picking and grinning. During pro football training camps, I had friends such as Willie Nelson and the Gatlin Brothers perform for my players. Even the athletes from urban cities seemed at home among my country friends.

Mama was about 5-foot-2-inches tall, and she couldn't have weighed more than 110 pounds. She was tough, though.

"One weekend she went home and decided to take her stepmother and one of the younger children to the picture show in town," my sister, JoAnnette, said. "But a child got in the car before anyone else and released the brake. The car rolled downhill, hit a tree and bent the tie rod. Mama took the tie rod off, fired up the forge in the barn, heated up the rod, straightened it, put it back on and away they went to town."

I remember collecting wood with Mama and planting rows of carrots and potatoes. We visited in the cramped kitchen while supper brewed. She had dark brown hair, a round face and an easy-going nature. Mama, bless her heart, was so kind. She showed her affection a lot more than Daddy did. She could make you feel bad for doing something you shouldn't, and she didn't have to yell. When I got to pro football, the Oilers management faulted me for being too close to my players. I don't understand that. I was real close to my Mama. I loved her and did everything she asked me to do. My players were the same way and we're still close.

"She was always there to help somebody and Bum's the same way," JoAnnette said. "Mama died in 1996 and not a day goes by that I don't think about her. She was sick during those final years. One day, she fell and hurt herself and they took her to the hospital. I saw Bum sit by the side of her bed and he held her hand. He was patting her and loving her and telling her it's going to be alright. He was so sweet and kind. I'd never seen him that way, to the point of tears. He got his compassion from Mama."

Mama rarely discussed God, but she often read the Bible by candlelight at night. My parents didn't recite scripture to us, but they taught us to live by life's golden rules: Treat others like you want to be treated. Work hard. Don't lie, steal or cheat. I believed if I followed these rules, I'd go to heaven. It was only later in life I learned the path to God is through Jesus Christ.

If I learned compassion from my Mama, I got a few things from Daddy, too – namely you don't take what you don't earn.

Daddy was also Oail Andrew Phillips, but everyone called him Flip, which was easier to say with a mouthful of tobacco (5). He worked odd jobs and often seven days a week. He left home before I awoke and returned well after I fell asleep. He set the ground rules, explained why they were important and taught luck is made through hard labor. He never missed a day of work, but he couldn't afford to.

Daddy lived with a black-and-white world view. His views of life weren't colored by the erratic social mores of today. It helped that, like me, he was colorblind – literally.

He worked hard, did right by his neighbor and taught us to do the same.

Daddy could also make sentences with cuss words. He had hands big enough to deflate a grapefruit, fingers so thick he could point your way and force your belly to flip. He showed love by working hard. Hugs and encouragement didn't buy flour and sugar. He said if a man fails to discipline his children, he does them a great disservice. He believed a child should be seen, not heard, and he had no qualms about whipping us with a leather strap. When he told you to do something, you better darned well do it. Before each whipping, he explained what I did wrong, how I could correct the problem and thus why I must be punished. The whippings hurt, but I always deserved them. One time, I cried during Daddy's pre-whipping talk because I knew all too well a lashing was next. That lashing seemed less severe. So, I improvised – called an audible, you could say. I started crying before all whippings, which saved a fair amount of skin on my already-tender backside.

I could tell Daddy loved me, but I don't remember him saying so. I knew he loved me just by the way he treated me. I was the same way with my players. Maybe I didn't tell them straight out, but there's a different way of saying, "I love you."

Daddy died of emphysema in the 1970s, and he was sick in his last years, too. He never came to one of my pro football games, but he'd have been proud of the way I left the sport.

After taking the Oilers to back-to-back AFC Championship games in the late 1970s, I became head coach of the New Orleans Saints. I was friends with the team owner, John Mecom. I told him he'd be the last owner I ever worked for and I was about ready to return full-time to ranching. Then, one December, he said he planned to sell the team. I'd already worked long enough in the NFL to qualify for a comfortable retirement, and Mecom's decision was all I needed to say goodbye. The problem, however, was the sale wouldn't happen until May and I couldn't quit in May. Doing so would have forced the team to scramble with little time before the season opener to find a new head coach and staff.

So, I told the new owner, Tom Benson, I planned to quit the following year. When the time came, I walked into his office. I had three years left on a guaranteed four-year contract. If I quit then and there, I could have collected the remaining $1.3 million owed to me.

Benson said he didn't know if he could afford to pay a guy a salary for three years when I wouldn't be there to earn the paychecks. I grabbed the contract and in big letters wrote "VOID" on every page.

"Now you can afford it," I told him.

I never did collect the $1.3 million. I gave up a small fortune just to return to my cattle and to live by my Daddy's mantra: If you don't earn something, you don't deserve it.

I think Benson appreciated the gesture. Heck, it saved his bank account some. As a credit to him, he kept me on his insurance program all these years. He still pays all my premiums.

After my son, Wade Phillips, led the Dallas Cowboys into New Orleans in December 2009 and ruined his Saints' undefeated season, Benson called me to congratulate Wade and my family. Despite the disappointment he felt for his own team, Benson had nothing but kind things to say about my son.

Sure, I was the coach with the cowboy hat and boots. I like to think what I learned to wear on the inside, though, is what made me the coach and man I am. I never let any amount of money change what I believe in.

BUM LESSON: Keep your word.

I like what my former NFL tight end and friend Mike Barber tells to young men and women he mentors: "Keep it simple, stupid."

With this in mind, my first lesson to you is to keep your word. Sounds simple, right? You should tack those three one-syllable words to a mirror you pass by often. A person is only as good as his or her word. I always told my pro players to pay their bills on time. Avoiding late payments is the same as showing up for a meeting when you said you would. It's just the right thing to do. Keeping your word also carries over into other areas in life.

My wife, Debbie, offered some kind words regarding the subject.

"The reason Bum has kept so many friends is he has always kept his word," she said, leaning from her seat toward our dining room table. "That defines who you are. Either you're trustworthy or you're not. Do unto the Lord."

Whatever you say you're going to do, do it. Don't lie to yourself or to anyone else.

CHAPTER 2

THE HARDER WAY

"No discipline seems pleasant at the time, but painful. Later on, however, it produces a harvest of righteousness and peace for those who have been trained by it." – Hebrews, 12:11.

B efore I tell you how I stumbled into football as a youngster, I should first say it's probably no coincidence I grew up during the Roaring Twenties. I emerged boisterous and active just as the United States surfaced stronger after World War I. Jazz music blossomed. The country beamed with confidence. I spent my early days soaking in newborn moods, which were filled with hope, opportunity and optimism. Although the prosperity that trickled to much of the country missed my home in Orange County, the sentiments didn't.

Through hard work and spurred by my disciplined parents, I learned personal confidence, which you need in life. I wasn't cocky, but I began to trust I could accomplish anything in life if I just believed in myself and put my mind to something. This basic understanding propelled me toward success in many areas of life. This sort of confidence can be a bad thing, too. I didn't know then just how much more I could have accomplished had I leaned on God. I believed in Him, but I know now every success comes via His grace. I coached thousands of kids and young men. Think of how many fathers, sons, brothers and businessmen I could have helped further had I understood the importance of placing all your faith in Jesus Christ.

Illustrating my early confidence remains easier said than done. You'll have to take my word for it. My youngest sister wasn't born yet and my oldest sister and parents, God bless them, are long dead. There isn't anyone around from my childhood to tell you what I was like. Heck, I'm 86. Most people from my early days are in the ground now. Suffice it to say, I was forged of a hotter fire. I never met a person who intimidated me – or a challenge I felt I'd fail to meet. Even this kind of confidence can get rattled, though.

On Oct. 29, 1929, the stock market crashed and the Roaring Twenties curled up into the fetal position, whimpering. I was 6 years old. Although my family didn't invest, we were still surprised by the fallout that steamrolled our way. During the next few years, wave after wave of economic despair slammed into Texas' east coast and elsewhere. The Great Depression took root. In one week, the U.S. stock market lost $30 billion, which is equivalent to $378 billion in today's terms (1).

As a result, millions of Americans lost their homes, and they fled to shantytowns. Unemployment soared. Men, who based their personal value on their ability to provide, sank into despair or scrounged for jobs. By the time I turned 12, the look of worry on my father's face became a familiar one. Unemployed, Daddy moved us from Orange to nearby Beaumont. There, we lived with family. Joe Phillips, my paternal grandfather, lent us a modest, two-bedroom home located only blocks from his own. My aunt lived next door. During this great, cold despair, family surrounded me like warm insulation.

In its early days, Beaumont was also a cattle center. Much like Orange, the city teemed with the commercial off-shoots due to its location on a river. In this case, the Neches River fueled lumber and rice mills. With nearby Port Arthur and Orange, Beaumont formed the most bustling corner of the Golden Triangle, a regional and industrial hotbed. Nothing put Beaumont on the map, though, quite like the Spindletop oil discovery of 1901. It became the country's first major oilfield, and the city's population exploded (2). Companies formed during the boom's first year later became corporate giants Texaco, Gulf Oil Corp and Exxon. The Magnolia Oil Refinery, where I worked when I was in my twenties, became the city's largest employer (3). During the depression, however, I witnessed this rush of oil and prosperity fizzle like a wet firecracker.

For a short while, Daddy worked as a mechanic and shop foreman for Chevy Motor Company. When the shop went out of business, he lost his job. Fewer and fewer consumers could afford automobiles, and those who drove largely opted against paying for repairs. During the next several months, Daddy worked as a dairyman and at a variety of other odd jobs. Soon, however, he found himself unemployed again.

One day, Daddy and I hopped a train from Beaumont to Lafayette, Louisiana. We didn't have a car or the money for two seats on a passenger train, so we sneaked onto a coal train headed east. I insisted we climb into a packed coal car so I could stand atop the blackened briquettes and stare at the foreign countryside. I wanted to search for the Indians I was certain roamed the scrubby brush. Of course, Daddy wouldn't allow it. We hopped into an empty coal car. If the men who checked for unwanted visitors spotted a boy's head peeking over the steel ledge, they'd throw us both off. Daddy needed to reach Louisiana. Claude Phillips, my uncle, said he might have a job offer.

When we reached Lafayette, my uncle picked us up at the train depot. Uncle Claude was a station manager for a motor freight company. Daddy wanted to ask for a job in person. I remember my uncle's 124-year-old home, the bedrooms that draped the long hallways and the sheer size of the place. The house was much larger than any house I'd ever lived in, and it sat on concrete pylons – above the ground and the depths of a typical flood. I played with my cousin, Jack Phillips, in the dry dirt underneath the house. Daddy rolled the dice inside, and the trip proved successful. We returned to Beaumont on the coal train the next day, and Daddy reported for work as a driver for T.S.C. Motor Freight Lines.

Grandpa Joe Phillips went on interstate trips of a different kind. He was once a Texas Panhandle cattleman. He worked a dozen years along the famous Goodnight-Loving Trail during the 1860s and 1870s. Grandpa Phillips blazed new trails much like I later did during World War II and in football.

The trail Grandpa Phillips, Goodnight and Loving blazed spanned more than 2,000 miles from Texas to Wyoming (4). The trail spanned from Young County, Texas, southwest to Horeshead Crossing on the Pecos River, northward to Fort Sumner, New Mexico, through Colorado and into Cheyenne, Wyoming. Goodnight and Loving wanted to capitalize on growing cattle markets. To cash in, they traveled across hostile Indian country and often moved 2,000 head of cattle with 18 riders. Grandpa Phillips made a name in the rough country for his skills on a horse and with a pistol. After returning from the trail, he settled in Beaumont to work as a master carpenter and as a foreman at a lumber yard.

After school most days, I returned home, told Mama about my classes and rushed to grandfather's house. During each visit, he told stories about life on the trail, showed me his worn pistols and painted a vivid picture of the work required to finish long journeys. The reality of it was the men who moved cattle from Texas to Wyoming endured great hardship and pain. There was no romance to it. It took forever to get where you were going and it wasn't a lot of fun. It wasn't as admired then as it is now. You had dust, weather and dirt for a bed. Grandpa's stories prepared me for the long hours I'd spend as a football coach. If I became tired while studying film – which I often viewed until the early hours of the morning – I'd think of Grandpa Phillips. He wouldn't stop or complain, and so neither would I.

My family's thrifty lifestyle, my father's work ethic and Grandpa Phillips' tales of endurance weren't the only life-changing experiences I absorbed during the Great Depression. Had the economic collapse not forced my family from Orange to Beaumont, I might not have gravitated to football.

I entered middle school as a seventh grader about the same time my youngest sister, Jo Annette, was born. My parents suddenly added one more hungry mouth to feed. Although I became accustomed to eating corn flakes three meals a day, I never complained because I always had enough to eat. God tests you during hard times to prepare you for His blessing. To this day, I don't need fancy food. During an August 2009 preseason trip to San Antonio to watch Wade coach the Dallas Cowboys, I dined at a popular Italian restaurant. A handful of those at the table ate calamari as a noontime appetizer. I looked at the expensive dish, shook my head and grabbed a long, uncut bread loaf. I broke it in two and spread butter on an open end. I learned as a boy to enjoy simple pleasures, and so today I also live debt free. If I can't buy something with cash, I figure I can't afford it. I can afford calamari, but I still prefer ribs, jalapeno-cheddar soup or a warm piece of bread.

I didn't give much thought to fancy food or money as a seventh grader. My eyes were suddenly opened, however, to a world that led me unknowingly to vast riches. One day, while the heat of summer still blanketed East Texas, I heard a yell in the school hallway.

"Who wants to play football?" someone said.

I raised my hand. "I will."

I'd never seen football or even heard about it, but my early days in the sport reveal a boy destined to become a coach. I told my coaches I was a running back, but I didn't know what the position entailed. I just wanted to play running back because everyone said I'd get the ball. Evidently, I was better than everyone because I started all the games – and newspaper reporters wrote flattering stories. I don't want to sound like I'm bragging, but I've always succeeded no matter what I did. I was captain of the first team I ever played on and I'd never played a down of football. I was tougher than all of the other players, too. Because my school had very few students, I played on offense and defense. When I didn't smash into tacklers, I delivered crunching hits as a linebacker.

Daddy, however, grew up playing baseball. He didn't like or understand football. He didn't believe a future existed in a game where a boy could break a leg in a snap. Broken legs meant doctor visits, medical bills and idle time away from work. Daddy didn't believe a boy should do anything to jeopardize his ability to help out where needed, and understandably so. Luckily, he remained employed during my middle school years, and thus he wasn't around when I returned home late from football practice. That changed, painfully so, when I graduated to the ninth grade.

During my first years at French High School, Daddy drove trucks from Beaumont to Houston twice a day, six days a week and on some Sundays. The pay: $12 a day. Like my father, I awoke early in the morning, ate a modest breakfast – an egg, milk and bread – and left for work at 4 a.m. I said goodbye to Mama, left behind the comfort of my warm bed and walked the town's streets toward the train station. By 1937, I was 14 years old and able to work a man's job. I worked in the train yard to help Daddy keep food in the cupboards and to pay for those things a freshman in high school might want. If I wanted a bicycle, I had to earn it.

Once at work, the smell of salty air and the sounds of seagulls filled my senses. Grown men who were hungry, cranky and bearded, stood in line to accept any job. Before the sun rose above the flat horizon line, the men gathered, sometimes fought and always hoped a freight car foreman would pluck him from the crowd. I had lied about my age – said I was 18 – to be eligible for work, and somehow the foreman always picked me. I worked for 30 cents an hour unloading freight cars at a frantic pace. If a worker moved slowly, dozens of strong men lined the tracks in wait. I could move like a nimble-footed running back, so I quickly unloaded freight cars and impressed my bosses. After three hours of this, I shook the dirt from my clothes, checked my short-cut hair and strode into class by 8 a.m. I kept this schedule for four years. After school each day, I then clamored to the football field.

At the beginning of the season, practices ran later than usual. Coaches used long days to whip us into shape. The unforgiving Texas sun, which has its own way of whipping a boy into shape, still shined brightly beyond dinnertime. During a lull in Daddy's truck-driving work, he struggled to find a replacement job. So, he was in the living room early one night when I returned home from practice.

"Why are you late?" Daddy asked.

"Football practice," I said.

"You quit that," he said. "You'll get your leg broke."

Stubborn-headed, I returned home late again the next night. Daddy asked me where I'd been. I said football practice and he wore my butt out good. Next night: The same thing. Daddy was like a lot of country people. He wanted you to do all the things you were supposed to do, and football wasn't one of them.

By the third night, Daddy's belt left a fleshy tattoo on my backside. The belt did the same on the fourth night. On the fifth night, he changed his approach.

"If you break your damned leg, it's your fault," he said. "Just remember I told you so."

He whipped me one more time, and then threatened me with a more painful punishment.

"This is the last time," he said. He clenched his fist, suggesting he'd punch me if I disobeyed his order again. "Next time will be this."

Daddy finally realized punishing me wouldn't stop me from playing football. I loved it too much. Certainly, he had the tools to scare a boy straight. His hands were large enough to engulf a football. His fingers were paper-weight thick and calloused like a cliff stone. He had the biggest hands I've ever seen, bigger than the claws my offensive linemen in Houston used to move large defenders. Daddy never punched me, though. In turn, I never got hurt, never broke a bone playing the sport. I played running back and linebacker in high school and college, and avoided the hospital like I did would-be tacklers. After high school, I competed in rodeos and left arenas unscathed. I survived explosive battles during World War II with nothing more than questions about why we fight. Ironically, the only time I seriously hurt myself occurred while riding atop a work horse, a symbol of the ranch and the way of life Daddy knew so well.

After leading the University of Louisiana to a college basketball championship, Coach Elbert Pickell moved to Beaumont. The 6-foot-2-inch, 190-pound man strutted like the successful college football and basketball player he'd been, and the winning coach he'd become. He found a home at French High School in the early 1930s. His jet-black hair, long face, sloped forehead and businessman approach spoke volumes before he ever uttered a word. Pickell was my first influential football coach, and he became the first man outside my patriarchs to shape my life for the better.

As a college basketball player, Pickell was part of the Arkansas Razorbacks' first conference championship team. In 1926, Arkansas went 23-2, won the Southwest Conference and Pickell played a major role in the success (5). In Beaumont, success rested on his shoulders once more.

Because he lacked assistants, Pickell coached every position, and he was good at them all. He was also good at teaching life lessons. He influenced me more than my Daddy because it's often easier for a high school coach than it is for a parent to communicate with a kid. Coaches are more important than people believe.

There wasn't any monkey business with Coach Pickell. He didn't care if you liked him or not, but I looked up to him. He led me in the right direction, and his ideas of right and wrong became my own.

I'd like to think I impressed Pickell, too. I earned a starting spot my entire high school career. I stood 5-foot-11-inches tall and weighed 160 pounds. The only player to weigh more was Theodore Jett. Despite my corn flake-heavy diet, I packed on more solid weight than most of the team's offensive linemen.

Because Beaumont's population dwindled when the Great Depression plugged the overflowing rush of oil, only 14 boys suited for the football team. One boy was courageous, but he had a crippled foot and never played unless we had an insurmountable lead. So, we had only two substitutes, which Coach Pickell rarely used. Once a player subbed out, he couldn't reenter. I never did spend too much time on the sideline and my parents spent even less time in the stands. Daddy watched only one game in person during my entire football career, including those years I coached in the NFL.

During my senior year in high school, we lost a preseason game 12-26 to Hull-Daisetta, our rival. We fought back, though, won every regular-season game and pushed for the regional championships. By the time we reached the playoffs, we were undefeated. To become champions, French High School had to face our nemesis once more. Hull-Daisetta was up next on the schedule.

Beaumont buzzed with excitement. Barbershops filled with the talk of a championship run. Merchants draped banners downtown and pinned encouraging signs to their storefronts. Football and winning were always big in Texas. Football was bigger per capita than it is now. They shut the town down when you played football. This was a big game.

Football became so competitive that coaches lured talent from nearby towns. Families moved from one city to another on the promise of a winning sports program. To combat what the high school governing body felt was tampering, a new Texas rule was initiated: Players who moved from their hometown must sit out the next year, thus lose a season of eligibility. The rule wasn't altered for decades. When Wade, my firstborn, played high school football for me, he lost two years of eligibility because I accepted two jobs in different towns. Coaches wanted to win at all costs, and the same fervor rushed through me as the game against Hull-Daisetta approached.

During the week leading up to this rematch, I tossed and turned, sick in bed. With an important game looming, not even a fever and nausea could keep me from the field. At 7-0 in district play, we all had revenge on our minds and an eye fixed on the crown.

For the first time, my father sat in the stands.

I'd like to think I displayed a gutsy performance during the first half. I ran the ball hard, picked myself up after each tackle and tried to forget the fever that burned inside my helmet. By halftime, we had a slim lead. Daddy walked down from the stands, right up to me and stared me dead in the face.

"Are you still sick?" he said.

Maybe he simply wanted to know if I felt ill after a week in bed. Maybe he tried to motivate me for the second half. Chances are he probably had work on his mind. If I could play football, I could unload freight the next morning.

We defeated Hull-Daisetta 9-7 that night and earned a first-place finish in the regional championships. My father wasn't impressed. He never said a word about the game or my performance.

Even so, he taught me hard work. Grandpa taught me resilience. Football taught me to work hard even when you don't feel like it. These lessons proved invaluable, especially during my next stop in life. After high school, I headed to war – and the good Lord tested me in every way imaginable.

BUM LESSON: Perform work heartily.

One Saturday afternoon, I sat with my wife, Debbie, at the dining room table. We discussed the importance of hard work. About that time, Debbie started talking about performing even the smallest task – sweeping the kitchen, for example, or pulling weeds in a garden – with an ethic that makes God proud. "He also learned to do everything he did with great passion," Debbie said, reading Colossians from the Bible. "And whatever you do, do it heartily, as to the Lord, and not to men."

I like that second part, I told her. You don't just do it, you do it heartily.

God always watches and He rewards you for working heartily for Him. Whether you're coaching a pro football team or answering phone calls for your boss, do the job well. In doing so, you honor God. My grandmother used to say, "Give it your best and then a little bit more."

CHAPTER 3

WAY TOO LONG

"How long, O Lord? Will you forget me forever? How long will you hide your face from me?" – Psalm 13:1

I don't deserve a whole lot of ink for my efforts in the war. Almost 70 years later, a man can invent heroic acts and nobody could dispute them. I was no hero. The guys who died fighting are the real heroes. Now that I'm 86, I've had a whole lot of time to enjoy our country. Many of those 19-year-old kids I fought alongside, on the other hand, didn't get to. I just did what I had to do, and I'd do it all the same. I feel it's everyone's obligation to protect your country.

It's important to detail this chapter of my life because in the military I matured, learned I couldn't whip everybody and discovered principles I'd use as a coach. In fact, I witnessed an event that almost magically pushed me later into coaching. Most importantly, I found God plants people and events in your life that draw you to Him, even if you aren't ready at the time to comprehend the signs.

When the Empire of Japan attacked Pearl Harbor, Hawaii, on the morning of Dec. 7, 1941, I reacted like most Americans. I became angry. I saw the images: the sunken U.S. Navy battleships, cruisers and downed airplanes. More than 2,400

Americans died during the surprise attack, and I was instantly eager to enlist – despite my mother's misgivings. She refused to approve sending her only son into battle.

Even so, I drove to San Antonio and enlisted with the U.S. Marine Corps on Sept. 30, 1942 – the day after my 19th birthday. I left Beaumont's Lamar Junior College as a freshman and headed for war.

The fog of war blurs with time. I don't remember clear details about my full tenure in the South Pacific, partly because I didn't look back after the war and partly because not every survivor wants to. War is, of course, the ugliest of human inventions. I would just as soon forget it. During the war, though, certain events and people imprinted memories on me like fresh footprints on a Guadalcanal beach. Not even time can wash those away. God works in mysterious ways, and He surely found a faraway place in which to labor in my life.

For a young, small-town South Texas man, the train ride to California for boot camp invigorated me. Never before had I traveled west farther than Liberty, a small town 45 miles from Beaumont. I passed cities and countryside I'd never seen, and visited with others from across the state. I knew where we were headed, and I couldn't wait to get there. I didn't think they could win the war without me. Everybody felt that way.

The Allied invasion of Normandy was still two years away, but tensions already brewed in the South Pacific. Island chains were key staging grounds, and both U.S. and Japanese war strategists eyed the areas with worry and lust.

Camp Pendleton, created on 122,798 acres to train U.S. Marines, was established just months before we arrived. The camp was the largest Marine Corps base in the country (1). Nestled along the California shoreline, it offered ideal training grounds for amphibious assaults. The coast didn't boast jungles, but it had heat, mosquitoes and beaches. Where we were headed, we needed to know how to dismount a Higgins boat, storm a beach in choppy water and stay alive in the process. Those boats, which Gen. Dwight Eisenhower later said won the war, were 36 feet long and could carry 36 combat-equipped infantrymen or 8,000 pounds of cargo (2). The large, hinged ramp on the boat's nose could drop on the sand like a gray welcome mat. Andrew Higgins, a Louisiana entrepreneur, created those boats. Like E.W. Brown – the man who gave my maternal grandfather a job on the ranch – Higgins began in the lumber industry. He built his boats of plywood, which was likely milled near my hometown.

I stepped foot inside Camp Pendleton as a bright-eyed and brash country boy. The six-week boot camp and yelling began at once. Never before had anyone treated me quite like those aggressive drill sergeants did. They taught us to obey commands, but no one ever explained why. I was ready to fight. I didn't need a stranger spitting in my ear to remind me of that.

During boot camp I learned the best way to get someone to do something is to explain why you need it done. I didn't learn the true meaning of taking orders, at least for the purposes used in the military, until after the war. If they said get your gun and go, well you got your gun and went.

I also became a skilled rifleman. I excelled at the range. As a private, I received a marksman weapons qualification on Nov. 23, 1942, and a special qualification as a truck and tractor driver. During the war, I bulldozed roads as part of reclamation work in the far South Pacific. Later in life, I cleared almost every square inch of the brush that cluttered my 250-acre Goliad, Texas, ranch.

At the end of the six-week boot camp, we marched to a building where the Marine Corps required men to choose their specialty. At first, I wanted to become a paratrooper, to drop behind enemy lines and to use my skills as a marksman – until

I saw the line gathered to join the unit. I hate long lines. When I was head coach of the Houston Oilers, I installed an extra 90-gallon fuel tank on my truck and stocked 500 gallons of diesel near the horse stables. This way, I didn't have to wait in line at gas stations. In the 1970's, I told a reporter that one of the hardest things for me to do is to sit in a barbershop and wait for a haircut (3). I won't do it. If I go by the barbershop and somebody's in the chair, I'll just keep going down the road. I'm not going to stand in line to eat or get a haircut. Therefore, I get real hungry and my hair gets long sometimes.

Instead of waiting in line to become a paratrooper, I walked to the line for the U.S. Marine Raiders, which was much shorter and for good reason. To join the Raiders a man had to stand 6 feet tall, weigh a certain amount and agree to perform much of the dirty work ahead. I entered the military as a solid young man, but I stood only 5 feet, 11 inches tall. Either I grew some during my six weeks on the coast or my ability to lead men accounted for an inch in the eyes of the Raiders.

While standing in line, I met David Van Fleet, a South Texas man who towered above us all. He stood 6-foot-5-inches tall and near the front of the line. At 210 pounds, he also caught the eye of a superior.

"Can you stand to get knocked on your ass?" the superior asked Van Fleet.

"I don't know. Never been knocked on my ass," Van Fleet said.

"You will get knocked on your ass," the superior replied.

"That remains to be seen," Van Fleet said, motioning to the officer as if to entice a fight.

I liked Van Fleet instantly. I knew right then, we'd be buddies.

My sister remembers being back home with my family, waiting and worrying. "When the Marines sent Bum's clothes home, Mama took the T-shirt he was wearing when he left and hung it on the headboard of the bed where it stayed the entire time he was gone," Jo Annette said. "Bum wrote home and told us he was joining the paratroopers and Mama was in tears. Wrote him back and begged him not to. He wrote back later, told Mama not to worry, that he had thought about it and was going to join the Raiders. Obviously, he felt that would make us all feel better."

With a war inevitable in the South Pacific, President Franklin D. Roosevelt ordered the creation of the U.S. Marine Raiders. The president wanted special amphibious attack forces, highly-specialized units like the British Commandos, who operated behind enemy lines. We were organized, armed and trained to fulfill three primary missions. The U.S. Marine Raiders Association states we were trained to:

⊠ Carry out surprise landings and hard-hitting raids on short notice from submarines, destroyers and other transports.
⊠ Infiltrate enemy lines and conduct guerilla warfare for extended periods.
⊠ Spearhead major amphibious landings where approaches were difficult and beaches confined.

We were also trained for amphibious reconnaissance missions using native transports, such as hollowed canoes. We wanted to hit hard and suddenly.

Immediately, my battalion of Raiders moved from Camp Pendleton to an installment just north of San Clemente, a California city located about 100 miles north of San Diego and a stone's throw from the Coastal Highway.

I joined the 4th Marine Raiders, the last of four battalions designated on Oct. 23, 1942. I served in Company D and

Q. Lt. Col. James Roosevelt, son of the American president, commanded my group. Roosevelt greeted us each time with a yell: "Ahoy, Raiders." During Roosevelt's first meeting, he made it clear that everyone would carry a weapon at all times. We slung our rifles across our backs during meals, and only set them aside during hand-to-hand combat training. I grew fond of jujitsu training. After three weeks, leaders separated my group from the others and moved the battalion to the boondocks, a place we called Tent Camp III.

Van Fleet, who is now 87, remembers the isolation of the battalion. "There wasn't a darned thing out there," Van Fleet said. "They didn't put us in barracks in the base and train us. We lived in tents. The floors were dirt. No lights and it was dark out there. We didn't even have any vehicles. We didn't have any plumbing facilities. We showered on a hill with no hot water. We'd go up on the side of that hill, bathe and walk back naked as a jaybird, and it was winter. Freeze your butt off. Got dirty a lot and they expected you to shower a lot. So, we spent a lot of time naked on a hill."

When we weren't shivering down a hill, we took cross-country marches. We marched on the highway and with very little water. We walked and walked and walked. The Army marched 49 miles in 10 hours, so we marched 55 miles in 10 hours. As soon as the 10 hours were up, we quit marching. We marched faster than any unit and I never got tired. I could have walked all night as far as I was concerned. I was used to exercise because I played football.

Van Fleet remembers those marches, too. He remembers the heavy loads we carried on our backs.

"After we shipped off, they'd drop us off on one side of an island and we'd walk across to the other," he said. While he said doctors disagree with him, Van Fleet blames those long walks on the neuropathy he developed 20 years ago. Neuropathy is a deterioration of the nerves that carry messages between the spinal cord and extremities. "My feet died. I can't walk at all now, not even a step. I got one of those mechanized wheelchairs. Been out of the Marine Corps 65 years and I haven't been sick a day. About 20 years ago, I started stumbling, falling. Maybe I wore my feet out."

Jerry Beau is a 92-year-old U.S. Marine Raiders historian. I never met the Wisconsin native because he served with the 3rd Raider battalion as a major. He said those long marches along the California coast served another purpose.

"We were a light assault force. The heaviest thing we had was a light machine gun," Beau said. "We had to walk forever because during the war we'd scout, take prisoners, do night work. We had to be a potent force, a special group."

To form into a feared light assault force, we trained long and hard. Day after day, we boarded destroyers, crammed into troop compartments, went to sea and returned in Higgins boats. We slipped ashore in calm California waters, and practiced landings during high surf. We moved by day and at night, practiced landing quickly, hiding the boats and securing areas along California tree lines. We patrolled, learned how to use our bayonets and to Abiscale.

President Roosevelt visited the West Coast one day not long before the 4th Raiders shipped to the South Pacific. He sat in a car atop a cliff overlooking the shoreline, and looked approvingly at our daytime beach landings.

During the few nights we didn't train, Van Fleet, Runt Brown and I talked by the camp fire. Runt died a few years ago, but I'm still friends with Van Fleet. We visit every few months. He's a big storyteller and does most the talking. Around the campfire, he talked about hunting and horses – everything but politics. I've known him for about 70 years and I still haven't figured out if he's a Republican or Democrat. He gripes about them all. After football, I helped campaign for both a Republican and Democratic Texas governor candidate. I flew around with Anne Richards when she ran against George W. Bush. I don't think I helped her much. She lost.

During our off time, Van Fleet and I played touch football or hopped trains to Los Angeles.

"We were kind of the same characters," Van Fleet said. "We both had played football for a semester in college. We're both pretty independent. We was cut the same way, you know. We weren't there to please people and get promoted. Bum got his self into more trouble than me. In the service, you're supposed to say, 'Yes, sir. Yes, sir.' We didn't go for that bull crap."

The night before we shipped out for the South Pacific, Van Fleet and I took a trip that later landed us in a makeshift military jail. We boarded a train again bound for Los Angeles. We caroused, mingled with the local women and enjoyed civilized life one last time before heading to the muddy jungles. The problem was we were supposed to return to base by 6 a.m. About midnight, we went to the train station but the seats were all full. So, we walked to the bus station. It was full, too. Finally, we headed to the highway and hitchhiked in. We got in about 7 in the morning – an hour late. Our superiors couldn't punish us then and there. They waited until we reached the first of many islands we'd visit during our tour.

A few hours after hitchhiking to camp, I stood on the shoreline with 3,000 other men. On Feb. 8, 1943, our stateside training was complete. I boarded the U.S.S. President Polk, a Marine transport. Two boilers were removed to make room for additional men. Van Fleet and I slept below deck in rooms with cots stacked five high. The space between each cot left just enough room for a Marine's nose to point upward. The transport lacked air conditioning. Poor ventilation to the lower decks made us sweat and stink, and we were angry. It was crowded, and it took forever to get there. We were like sardines in a can.

The ship crisscrossed the Pacific Ocean to avoid enemy submarine attacks, sailed beyond Hawaii and continued southwest toward New Hebrides, an island chain about 800 miles northeast of Australia. Two Raiders wrote music and spent hours belting tunes from a small spinet piano during the seemingly endless voyage. Despite the mind-numbing boredom onboard, we were excited to finally be at sea. When we crossed the equator and the International Date Line, we joked about going to bed one night and waking up yesterday. We gathered at the ship's rails, marveled at the sea's deep blue tones and stared into its smooth, glassy appearance. The ship sliced through the water for more than 6,000 miles, and the trip lasted 29 days.

We landed in Espirtu Santo, New Hebrides Islands, a staging ground for a push north and through the Japanese stronghold of island chains. I went to shore in a Higgins boat. While the rest of the Raiders established a base camp, superiors ordered Van Fleet and me to set up the jail.

"Supposedly, they was punishing us for coming in late that day we shipped off," Van Fleet said. "The jail was a tent. We each had a cot. A guy guarded us. We spent three days in that jail."

After being released from jail, we continued to rehearse boarding and unloading Higgins boats – only now along the various small, foreign islands. While going ashore, natives often approached us with baskets of breadfruit, papaya and taro root.

While on New Hebrides, I met Father Paul James Redmond, the battalion's chaplain. Redmond was a 44-year-old Connecticut native, and he'd already served during World War I. One day, we crept along a log, which other Marines chopped down and positioned so we could cross a washed-out ravine. Father Redmond slipped and I caught him, grabbed the skinny man by the collar and saved the chaplain from a dangerous fall. He stood, reached the other side and asked me if I'd become his personal bodyguard. I told him I would. I didn't go to his services during the war, however, because Christianity wasn't important to me then. Still, I did whatever he needed.

The Chicago Daily Tribune details Redmond's most famous rule-bending story, although he has many. A Jan. 26, 1961, newspaper story details the chaplain's piano theft. Redmond and my battalion sat in the mud of the New Hebrides Islands awaiting orders to spearhead the invasion of New Georgia. Redmond knew the Raiders had several good piano players. A Navy transport in the harbor had a good piano but no pianists, the article notes.

Redmond thought a piano was a great morale builder for his men. A great storyteller, he boarded the transport at nighttime, stood on the quarterdeck and talked to the Navy men. A few unidentified Raiders sneaked onboard, beyond the quarterdeck, down the ladder and onto a rubber boat with a bulky package covered by a tarpaulin. Redmond ran interference while the Raiders stole a piano.

According to the 1961 article, Redmond said, "I told them to hide it where I would not know where it was. Where do you think they put it? Under the altar in my makeshift chapel."

I deny any part in the theft, but I never forgot what Father Redmond did. He gained our confidence and respect. He was a priest who also joined us in battle. He crawled through enemy lines to administer last rites to wounded Marines, and he risked his life to gather dog tags from the dead. Some say he personally buried 3,000 Marines and one third of my battalion alone.

In 1960, 15 years after the war, Father Redmond began ministering in prison, a calling I also later followed. He lived into his nineties. He's now rightfully buried in Arlington National Cemetery.

"I don't know what kind of scrap he got into, but Father Redmond always tried to get Phillips out of the trouble he was in," Van Fleet said. "Phillips stayed with him for quite some time."

We moved north and up the slot of islands. We island hopped for a few months and formed bases along the different chains. We began surrounding Japanese strongholds in an effort to cut supply and ammunition lines. We built our company headquarters along one of these chains on a low ridge that sloped toward the beach. Coconut trees abounded. We followed a simple rule: Drink from the coconuts you snatch from a tree and eat the ones found on the ground. When the rain fell in buckets, we rejoiced. Rain meant a break from the heat, but we knew the ground would soon flood. Water oozed into our tents and deposited an ever-nagging sludge on everything. Physical ailments began to mount. A lack of regular food, a rain-induced infestation of mosquitoes and long days spent training and fighting began to take a toll. I suffered from fungus infections, the shakes, malaria, jaundice and yellow fever. My weight dropped dramatically.

While we fought the Japanese and the nuisances of jungle life, I tried to remain in contact with my family back home, although all my letters were censored.

"So, this is the way Bum devised to let us know where he was: He signed a letter, 'Your son, N.H. Phillips' and it got past the censors," JoAnnette said. "Mama and Daddy figured it meant 'New Hebrides Islands.'"

On March 22, 1943, we moved to an advanced base at Tetere, Guadalcanal, to prepare for a fight in New Georgia in the Solomon Islands. First, we took Vanguna Island. From

June 28 to July 10, 1943, we engaged in the first of many battles against the Japanese.

The clear night sky seemed perfect for the invasion of Vanguna, an island just south of New Georgia. Problems, however, brewed beneath the surface. An underwater storm created swells 20 feet high and loading into the Higgins boats turned into a deadly struggle. The swells, which heaved and rolled the Higgins boats, forced us to time our jumps just right from the nets dangling down the side of the destroyer. If we waited too long, the Higgins boat dropped 20 feet below. If we jumped too soon, the Higgins boat rose high above our heads. There wasn't any second try. If you missed it, you went missing. We lost three guys before we ever made it into the boats.

Luckily, I loaded into my boat just fine. I stood on the destroyer platform, reached overboard and grabbed the netting. Slowly, I climbed down it, keeping a boot and hand tight against the rope. Just before the Higgins boat began its steep ascent, I jumped and met it halfway to the top of the swell. I landed in the boat with a thud, but at least my feet touched wood and not saltwater. The trip toward the beach, however, had just begun. A few hundred yards offshore, our boat became stuck on a coral reef. We rocked it from side to side to free it and the reef damaged our propeller.

My eyes struggled to adjust to the darkness. The destroyers in the distance bobbed in the water. Men in Higgins boats pushed toward the shore in all directions. We didn't know where we were. We hollered, "Hoe. Hoe." We made a lot of noise we shouldn't have made, but we got off in four heaves and floated the rest of the way in.

Storm waves kept us from docking on the beach and we unloaded into the choppy water. Ben, a friend, crushed his leg between solid, heaving masses when he jumped from the destroyer to the Higgins boat, and Van Fleet carried him through the shallow waters and to the island.

"He was a big ole boy," Van Fleet said. "Weighed a ton. I asked him, 'Why'd you stay in the Higgins boat if your leg was broken?'"

"I didn't think I could make it back on the destroyer," Ben said.

Luckily, the Japanese didn't see the invasion coming, and thus didn't fire one shot during our landing. I reached the shoreline and joined a small group and a guide. We marched in the shadows, deep into the jungle and finally neared the Japanese camp. We attacked it. During a 14-day battle, we destroyed the enemy's radio facilities, supply depots and eliminated the garrison. The raid distracted the Japanese from reinforcing the Guadalcanal with soldiers. Instead, the Japanese sent reinforcements to Vanguna, but their ships, struggling in the ocean's swells, became grounded. We dug in on the shoreline, hidden by steep, rocky crops or high atop the cliffs and lobbed hand grenades. They were sitting ducks. We pushed the occupying force into the ocean, and then we camped.

After securing the island, we transferred to an unoccupied section of Guadalcanal to restore our supplies. We had little food, less ammo and a short supply of energy. We needed a break. Most of us lived through what Winston Churchill said was life's most exhilarating moment: We were shot at and missed.

Our role in the war was far from over, though. Beau, the Raider historian, said that of the 8,600 Raiders in four battalions, 2,600 earned Purple Hearts and 1,000 were killed.

My Daddy whipping me several nights in a row for playing high school football served as a prelude to military downtime. During a break, I displayed quite the propensity for getting into trouble. I was there to fight, and if I wasn't fighting I seemed to find myself in a mess. Superiors wrote me up four times in one day. That might explain why I entered the war as a private and left with the same rank. I've always been a bit of a rebel, but you can only go so far before you should join them.

Awaiting orders one morning to invade New Georgia, we were anchored aboard a destroyer that floated between two islands. We weren't regularly fed like other units. During one stretch, I lived off chocolate bars for almost 10 days. Hungry, I grabbed a fellow Raider and we jumped overboard, splashing into the water 30 feet below. We swam 100 yards and toward the shoreline, carrying with us rucksacks and a taste for coconuts. Despite my gift as a swimmer, I underestimated the strong current and missed by 50 yards the landing spot near the coconut grove. When we finally reached the sand, we slinked into the jungle to collect the fruit, filled our rucksacks and returned to the water. This time, we walked 50 yards up the beach to account for the current. We waded into the water until the small waves slapped our chests. The coconuts bobbed beside us. Once our chins touched the water, we swam. The water was cool, refreshing. The sun shined bright. The coconuts, though, slowed our progress. The current seemed to salivate at the thought of tossing us farther out to sea. It swallowed us again and pushed us away from the destroyer. Realizing we couldn't swim against the water, we yelled and waved. Suddenly, we'd drifted 50 yards downstream of our ship, which taunted us from its anchored spot. Finally, a topside crewman spotted us and sent a rubber boat.

"We wanted to get some coconuts," I told the man. "So, we jumped over the ship and grabbed some."

When we reached the ship, my superior found my reasoning unacceptable. The captain scolded me and then filed a formal reprimand, my first of the day.

As part of the punishment, the captain ordered me to head below deck and to sweep the cramped bunk rooms. I hated sweeping rooms as much as I hated mowing grass. After cleaning the floors around a few bunks, I walked to a room where I found a man sleeping. I was upset because he wasn't supposed to be in there. So I asked him to move. When he wouldn't, I swept dust into a pile and then flipped the mound onto the man. The corporal, infuriated, forced me to join him in a visit with the captain. Fresh off a speech about why he disapproved of men who jump ship, the captain scolded me again and filed his second formal reprimand of the day. The captain looked up, asked me to acknowledge the significance of his signature and said I should find better ways to spend my downtime.

The sleepy-eyed corporal, though, still angered me. I turned to him and called him a tattletale in rougher terms and said I'd whip his butt as soon as we left. Before the ink dried on my second formal reprimand, I received another. It was barely noon, and the captain had already written me up three times.

The fourth reprimand of that lazy day should have come as no surprise. After finishing my janitorial punishment below deck, I wiped my brow, returned topside and squinted against the hot sun. I was off duty and yearning to cool myself. Instead of showering, I looked around. With no officers in sight, I removed my shirt, flipped my chain so that my dog tags dangled against my back and jumped over the ship's railing. I landed in the water and cooled instantly. I floated on my back, soaked in the diluted heat and kicked my feet. A man on deck, though, heard the splash.

"Hey, get back on here," he yelled.

I refused and the Raider onboard then pointed to his collar. He, like the man who'd signed three documents that day, was a captain. I found myself in an office facing a superior once more. The captain said, "Bum, that's four times in one day. Go find Van Fleet and your friends and stay out of trouble, wouldya?"

The night we left for New Georgia – June 20, 1943 – was as clear as the night we left for Vanguna, only this time a storm didn't swell within the seas. As it turned out, the storm awaited us inland. This battle would be the costliest and most challenging we faced the entire war. I was with the first wave of Marines during the assault. Allied coast watchers, who'd befriended natives, learned the Japanese wouldn't enter the landing area (4). Given an uncontested beach landing, our mission was supposed to be simple: break through the Japanese stronghold, gather intelligence and seize the Munda airfield. The landing would be unopposed, but the fighting inland would become fierce.

The Japanese captured New Georgia a year earlier and established an airbase at Munda Point, a location that offered the enemy support positions during fighting in the Guadalcanal. Once the Japanese realized they could no longer hold Guadalcanal, they retreated to New Georgia and fortified positions to fight the Allied push farther north. We sailed toward a hornet's nest. By June, the Japanese installed 10,500 soldiers on New Georgia and 9,000 others nearby. Each of the forces were dug in and waiting for us to show up. We didn't know it, but we were outnumbered 10 to 1 on New Georgia and 20 to 1 if you count the Japanese soldiers an island away.

The U.S. Air Force didn't carpet bomb the island before the ground invasion. Ships at sea didn't blast fortified positions to soften the defense. We, as we were trained, stormed the water by Higgins boat, the beaches by foot and the jungles by adrenaline and instinct. We lacked tanks, Jeeps and support from the north. The Allied plan was to hit the island with the Raiders from the south and with the Army from the north.

The Army, however, was a day late. Nobody bothered to tell me and my comrades.

The early morning sky was still black and cloudless. The moon shined bright. The salty water was calm and the stars glimmered in the rolling waves. I climbed down the netting on the side of the destroyer, slunk into the Higgins boat and adjusted my helmet. I wore all-green fatigues, carried an M-1 rifle and hauled a light pack. Four destroyers floated in the water, and I watched their outlines fade into the horizon as the Higgins boat crept quietly toward shore.

The Japanese were dug in, and they numbered far greater than what anyone expected. The twists and turns of their fortified positions formed a hand, and the Japanese placed special attention on a finger-shaped section. We landed on the island's south side, about five miles from the enemy. One thousand Raiders hit the beaches and began a methodical push north. Just as on Vanguna, we landed without receiving enemy fire. We pushed toward the enemy base through the thick, entangling jungle growth, around coconut trees, up and down ravines and through mangrove swamps. Because of frequent rainstorms, the ground was muddy. It caked to a man's rubber-soled boots and made his steps heavy. I could smell the rice in the flooded fields.

By daylight, we neared the enemy camp and the four companies spread out. The Japanese opened fire first. Enemy men, hidden in machine gun nests, trees and caves, and near boulders and other hideaways, rained down a storm of bullets. They knew where we were, but we couldn't see them.

The Japanese installed defensive lines a few hundred yards outside their camp in all directions. The line formed a fierce, protective bubble. This military wall, which blended into the dense jungle, at once pulsed red with bullet fire. Japanese machine gunners crossed their bullet sprays, which left little room for escape or movement.

We had four rifle companies, three rifle platoons – of which I was a member – and a weapons platoon. Van Fleet fought with the weapons platoon. Each Raider was equipped with a weapon – a rifle, machine gun or flame thrower – and each carried hand grenades and a Gung-Ho knife.

Once gunfire erupted, we spread out over a great distance and moved into an arched formation, which bowed outward at the middle. I smelled gunpowder, heard the mortar explosions landing all around and dodged the tree branches that fell from the fray above. I heard the order: "Move!" One by one, each 50-member group charged 10 steps forward, in waves, and then took cover. While on the ground, I scouted the thick tree line ahead. I couldn't see anyone. Without a tank, we were ill-equipped to penetrate the defensive wall. Our largest weapon, a 50-caliber machine gun, proved fruitless. I knew we were losing when I again heard the command to charge, and this time only 12 men pushed forward at a time. The charges grew shorter and shorter. The closer we got to the enemy base, the fiercer the fighting became. A concentrated fury of Japanese artillery and mortar fire poured down from the gun-studded mountain fortress, bullets dropping from the rocky ridges like a hail storm. The green, grassy terrain became a killing field. We didn't have time to think. We ran out of ammunition by about 3 p.m. and engaged in hand-to-hand combat with bayonets. Then, we had to pull back. We had no reserves and no ammunition. The Japanese had all the advantages. I was just thankful to be alive.

Many of my fellow Marines, however, were not so lucky. In four hours, two-thirds of the battalion became casualties of war. Men were ripped apart in explosions, killed by bullets and maimed by grenades and other shrapnel. When men fell to the ground wounded, we created makeshift stretchers by tying shirts to bamboo poles. We hauled 360 Marines out.

Soon, though, we lacked enough standing soldiers to carry every wounded man to safety. Already, 700 men were dead or wounded. Three went missing in action. Only one-third of my crew could fight, and the Japanese were taking it to us.

When leadership within the Raiders realized we could no longer advance, they ordered us to retreat a good distance south of the enemy base. Medics worked overtime. The commander gave us an option: Head to the beaches and return to the ships, or dig in and fight if the Japanese counterattacked. We voted to stay put. We set up camp and a defensive perimeter. I established a post, stood guard and became angry. I got real mad once I learned the Army didn't attack from the north as planned.

My role was just to survive that night, but I had time to think. I thought about how we sometimes ask people to do things during a war without thinking plans through. What I now know for sure is that God looked out for me. I struggled with faith at that moment, though, because it seemed there were a lot of people He didn't look out for. Watching them die planted questions in my head that went unanswered for years.

Luckily for us, the Japanese didn't counterattack. Maybe they gauged the ferocity of our initial attack and figured we had a few thousand men ready and waiting. Maybe the Japanese were on New Georgia temporarily and had no plans of staying put. Maybe something greater acted behind the scenes all along. If the Japanese would have counterattacked that night, no Raider with a grain of reason thinks he'd be here today. The Japanese could have rolled through the jungle and taken each of the 300 men left standing. But they didn't. The Army arrived the next day and attacked from the north. Combined with our efforts, U.S. forces began to overrun the island

and push the Japanese into the sea, even though the fight continued for weeks. I fought in the jungle and patrolled the waters just offshore.

Raiders killed in action were still in the field. Father Redmond said last rites to men who lived long enough to see his face, and he called on me once again. Redmond wanted to retrieve the dog tags off the 300-plus men who fell dead in the battle. He wanted to return to the battleground knowing full well enemy machine guns would be trained on us.

Redmond, me and two other Raiders crept again from the camp and toward the enemy base. First, however, the chaplain asked us to leave our rifles against a tree, to break the habit we'd been ingrained with since boot camp. We looked puzzled, worried. We trusted Father Redmond, however, and always did as he said. We set off into the jungle unarmed, walking through the trees to look for the bodies of Americans.

Van Fleet remembers my time at the priest's side. "He was always with that padre," he said. "That padre would just walk out there, machine guns firing, shooting like hell, and he'd just walk out there and pray. Bum would say, 'That son of a gun is going to get me killed.' He never left his side, though."

As we inched farther into the tree line, we stumbled across the bodies of fallen comrades. One by one, we pulled the dog tags from their necks, slipped them into a pocket and crawled north. There is no doubt the Japanese could see and hear us. It's amazing they didn't shoot. I promise you a bullet from a rifle can go farther than a voice, and they could hear us. We were so close – about 30 feet away – that we listened to them talk. Somebody looked out for us that day, and I didn't have anything to do with it. It took us hours, but we collected all the dog tags and sent each one back to the families. The Army later helped us retrieve all the bodies. All but three were found and given proper burials.

The fighting on New Georgia lasted a few weeks. On June 20, 1943, we moved to a place called Sergi Point. On June 30, we paved the way for the construction of an airfield, a strategic strip from which Allied air attacks could launch. We then captured a harbor and another airbase. By Aug. 25, 1943, the fighting was finished. During those tense weeks, we learned from the Army that, before the attack, members radioed the message they'd be a day late. Raider commanders pushed onward anyway.

That the Army had makeshift kitchens, stoves, eggs and meats didn't quell the contempt we held for them, but it did give Father Redmond an idea. For months, we had survived on sparse food – moldy chocolate bars, island scraps and little else. I'd entered the Marines at 200 pounds and now weighed 130. Father Redmond asked me to join him in the Jeep for a visit to the Army camp, which was quite a distance around the bend. Just as he'd done on the ship with the piano, the priest ran interference, this time telling stories about gun swaps. He promised Army officers rifles, swords and ammunition in exchange for food and juices. The Army bit. Father Redmond and I loaded the Jeep full of food and drinks, and we sped away. We joked that we'd "liberated" the Army's food, clothing and alcohol, which none of us had at the Raider camp. Many Marines, especially those with yellow jaundice, claimed their lives were saved by the fruit and juices the priest provided us. I know he saved my life.

In need of a break from battle, we shipped out of New Georgia and returned to Guadalcanal, where we replenished our supplies and received needed downtime. I was sick, though. I had malaria, jaundice, dingy fever and other ailments. When I learned my battalion received permission to rest and relax in New Zealand, I defied doctors' orders, left the hospital and vacationed anyway.

Once in New Zealand, we enjoyed steaks, eggs, chips and oysters. We drank cold beer, the kind that at once chills your throat, your stomach and the memories of a bloody battle. The people of Auckland were friendly, welcoming. They treated us with respect and admiration. After a two-week stay, we returned to action. We hopped islands again for months.

On Jan. 8, 1944, commanders disbanded the Raiders. Because of our heavy casualties, and the nature of the new war, those of us who still stood had outlived our mission. Light attack forces were no longer needed in large-scale amphibious assaults in the South Pacific. The 4th Raiders split. I joined with other Raiders to form a reclamation group assigned to the Russell Islands. I operated a bulldozer, plowed new roads and worked to make once teeming, beautiful islands inhabitable again.

In all, I spent six months in training, 18 months in combat and 11 months busy with reclamation work. My Marine discharge papers note I served in the South Pacific from Feb. 19, 1943, to April 21, 1945, the year the war ended. I finally boarded a ship in the Russell Islands bound for San Francisco. After I reached California, I hopped aboard a train headed for a military hospital in Norman, Oklahoma. I spent six weeks there in treatment for malaria.

"Mama, Edrina and I went there to meet the train," Jo Annette said. "I can't remember if Daddy went or not. Can't imagine him not going but maybe we couldn't afford it. We had to stay at someone's home because the motels were full. It was cold and we stood on that train platform trying to recognize him among all those other boys."

I was honorably discharged on Aug. 18, 1945, inside the military hospital. The Marines paid me $153.55, or 5 cents per mile in reimbursement fees for my return trip home to Beaumont. Van Fleet returned to his home in South Texas, too. Although we lived hundreds of miles apart, we never lost touch. Van Fleet was in the stands 30 years after the war when I coached the Houston Oilers. He stayed at my house during trips to see doctors to learn why his feet failed him. He still visits me in Goliad.

"He got into the coaching business and I got into the construction business," Van Fleet said. "You know, there are only 200 Raiders living still from all four battalions. Bum and I are the only two living in Texas."

Like I said before, I didn't look back after the war ended – except to recount my memories here. I don't see much reason to reminisce about war. During the 1980s, however, I spotted a newspaper ad while coaching the New Orleans Saints. The Raiders were to hold a reunion in The Big Easy. I traveled to a local hotel, asked the man at the front desk for Father Redmond's room number and rode the elevator to the priest's floor. I'm not much of a fraternity guy. I never went to a Raiders reunion, but I did go see Father Redmond. I'm just happy he remembered me. We laughed about a lot of things: stealing a piano and getting food on the promise of guns and swords. When it comes to the war, Father Redmond and Van Fleet are my only real pleasant memories. I also witnessed an event that almost inexplicably pushed me into coaching. Like I said before, God works in mysterious ways, and He surely found a faraway place in which to labor in my life.

BUM LESSON: There's a difference between griping and coaching.

I'm not here to second guess how the military trains its soldiers. I do have something to say about the best way to lead in civilian life. Simply put: If you gripe at everybody, you accomplish nothing. To motivate someone – whether it's a child, an athlete or a coworker – you have to explain why something needs to be done before you can ask someone to do it. Tell me why, and I'll do just about anything. I learned how to coach from being in the U.S. Marine Corps. I learned how *not* to tell somebody to do something. If you have to holler to get somebody to do something, they aren't listening or you aren't doing something right. Football coaches are notorious for hollering. You ask most any player, and I'll bet they agree on one thing: They work harder and more sincerely for coaches who avoid screaming and insults.

Andy Dorris played on my defensive line in Houston. After football, he started a successful construction company. Dorris said he learned a few things from me about leadership.

"Say you have a bunch of people in a 100-yard dash," Dorris said. "They mill about the starting line. Each person looks left and right, and everybody appears pointed in varying directions. Your job is to point them the same way and let them run. Get out of the way and just let them run. Sit back and enjoy it, and make sure they don't run out of bounds. Over-coaching is yelling at them while they're running."

CHAPTER 4

WHICH WAY?

*"Trust in the Lord with all your heart and lean not
on your own understanding; in all your ways acknowledge
him, and he will make your paths straight." – Proverbs 3:5, 6*

A t the time, surviving World War II and the battle
at New Georgia failed to persuade me God works
behind the scenes. Soon, however, I received other
reminders about how life unfolds along His path – and how
events along the way push you to places He wants you to go.
I didn't acknowledge this truth until years later.

I was discharged from the military hospital and the
Marines at the same time. When I returned to Beaumont in
1945, I embarked on a new adventure: earning a living without
a rifle. First, though, I treated my baby sister.

"I remember him buying me a wonderful doll, which I
only would look at since I never was into dolls," Jo Annette,
now 74, said. "This is the first he'll ever know that I never
played with it."

Jo Annette, I later learned, preferred checking fences on
horseback over girly impulses such as doll collecting. Likewise,
I entertained thoughts of breaking wild horses. I traveled
to West Texas – along the same route I journeyed during

the train ride to war – in search of deals on fine-but-feisty animals. I intended to find, break and sell them for good money.

"He also wanted to get into the cattle business," Jo Annette said. "Mama and Daddy sold their house where they had lived forever, and they moved. I seem to remember it was something Bum wanted to do, and they would have done anything he wanted."

To support my business idea, the family needed more land. Vidor, a small town just east of Beaumont, offered such space at a cheaper cost. I also leased 850 acres and a dairy herd, and worked it some. We sold our small house and bought another with room outside to stretch our legs. The wild horse business, however, wasn't as accommodating. I bought 2-year-olds, hauled them six or eight at a time to my parents' home and then sold them. The money, however, wasn't enough to provide a stable life at the time. After returning from the war, I was like most other young men and women of the day: My eyes were big, and my dreams were, too.

I traveled south for a bit to work alongside Van Fleet, my war buddy. I landed other odd jobs, too. I worked as a lineman – climbed poles in Louisiana – and ran wire near the Sabine River. I stared out at the horizon from my perch 80 feet in the air.

I also met a banker's daughter. Helen Wilson, who was born prim and proper in my hometown Orange, caught my eye. Her sister worked at a shipyard with my oldest sister, Edrina, and we instantly connected the day we met. I married Helen, my first of two wives, in a Methodist church in 1946. We were hopeful, young and attractive, and I don't mind saying so.

I was 23 years old, had a good-paying job and love was in the air. Soon, the smell of oil would change my family's life forever.

Who would have thought I'd become a coach because of a decision I made as a grunt laborer?

Because it was too late in the school year to rejoin college, I opted for a full-time job at the Magnolia Petroleum Company in Beaumont. It was the best job I could find at the time. Helen and I found a small home in nearby Orange and set out to start a new life together.

The Beaumont oil refinery, now known as Mobil, was one of the largest in the world. The refinery, as the name implies, took crude oil and refined it into more useful products such as gasoline, diesel fuel and kerosene. The refinery resembled a vast steel city, and the billowing smoke loomed like a Los Angeles haze. The refinery had hundreds of tanks stocked with crude. I was happy to work on the ground, to stand in the dirt and help the men who worked high above. The men dropped ropes and I'd tie the juiceless electric lines to one end, pull the rope hand over fist and send the lines upward so the overhead workers could connect them to the plant's power poles. I would have become a plant lineman, worked my way up to become a supervisor, but my days at Magnolia were numbered.

So, too, were my days as a childless husband. After the war, the country became home to a baby boom – and my household was no different. On June 21, 1947, Helen gave birth to my firstborn son, Wade Phillips. Like me, Wade was born in Orange and went on to become an NFL head coach. His arrival instantly made my good-paying job an even greater necessity. With two more children on the way within four years, my sole focus in life shifted to providing. This instinctual realization makes my choice to suddenly quit my job even more mysterious. I thought I'd stay at the Magnolia Oil Refinery until I retired. I probably would have, too, if not for an experience I had with the Red Cross in the South Pacific.

While fighting in the South Pacific, I watched repeatedly as a few Red Cross employees sold items to soldiers the nonprofit workers were tasked to give away. They sold cigarettes and candy to the servicemen instead of giving it away for free like they were supposed to. I didn't like it, it wasn't right, and I decided as a young soldier I'd never give one dime to the Red Cross.

Despite my misgivings, the Magnolia Oil Refinery's longstanding tradition called for each employee to donate one-tenth of one day's pay to the Red Cross.

While I worked near the base of a crude oil tank, my supervisor walked up to me.

"You need to sign this," he said.

I stared at the document, read the part about donating to the Red Cross and then thought for a second.

"I tell you what I'll do," I said. "Make it out to the Salvation Army – any other charitable group – and I'll sign it. Otherwise I'm not going to do it."

The supervisor stared at me, grabbed the document and walked away. He returned about a week later and asked me again to sign the form.

"I'm still not signing that thing," I said.

"You have to," my supervisor replied.

"No way," I told him.

After I refused, the supervisor then escorted me to the company president's office. For a moment, I remembered my time on the Marine destroyer, those four visits I paid to the ship's captain in one day.

The company president's office was as big as my house. Expensive-looking mahogany lined the walls. I looked at the silver trinkets, the sprawling desk and the executive's tailored suit. The president, who sat tall in his leather chair, told me if I didn't donate to the Red Cross, I'd lose my job.

"In that case, tell the man at the gate to have my check ready," I said. "I'm leaving."

The boss tried to persuade me to finish the week, to earn a proper paycheck. I refused. I left the office, marched down the hallway and toward the man at the front gate. I had a high school diploma, a newborn at home and, I'd like to think, the moxie to stand firm in my convictions. I got in my pickup and left.

I have since donated to the Red Cross. I learned years later those unscrupulous nonprofit workers who sold items meant to be free were involved in an isolated case and were not emblematic of the organization as a whole.

If I'd known that then, I might never have become a coach.

While the prospects of sudden unemployment didn't fully settle in as I drove off in anger, I would have rested much easier had I known this one choice would one day make me wealthy beyond most dreams.

Every day after work, I drove through the same parking lot exit, cruised down the same long road and turned right toward my Orange home. I did this every day without exception. This day, however, I exited the parking lot, cruised down the long road and then turned left instead of right. I had no reason at the time to do so. Maybe I wanted to clear my head, to rehearse the conversation with my wife. Looking back, I know now something much larger steered me down the path.

After turning left, I drove a short while and passed scenery – blossoming new development along the highway – I'd never seen. I zoomed by building after building. Then to my right a break formed in the commercial landscape. I spotted a football practice, the comforting, familiar vision of football players in pads. I slowed, turned into a dirt parking lot and stopped my truck. I stepped outside, crossed my arms and leaned against the hood.

Before the war, I played one season of football as a freshman for Lamar Junior College. Unbeknownst to me, the college had relocated to this patch just off the highway. The practice would have been held miles away just months before.

Ted Jeffries, the Lamar coach, noticed me watching practice from the parking lot, and he approached me.

"You a football player?" Jeffries said.

"Used to be," I told him. "I played for Lamar before I went to the war."

"Well, how would you like to play for me this year? You like to tryout for a scholarship?"

"What kind of scholarship?"

"G.I. Bill."

"I ain't got nothing better to do," I told him.

After a few practices, Jeffries gave me a full-ride, $120-per-month scholarship under the G.I. Bill, plus room, board and tuition. Additionally, I received $115 per month to pay the bills, feed my family and clothe little Wade. Better still, I found a new job within minutes of quitting another. Thirty minutes either way and I would have missed the practice.

Now, some might say this was just dumb luck. When you get to my age, though, you have the advantage of better sense. God planted those nonprofit workers in my life and the left turn on my path. I was on my way to a football career compliments of a misunderstanding about the Red Cross and God's ingenious way of shepherding his flock.

I played football for Coach Jeffries for one year and became the team's captain. Lacking the speed to play running back like

I did in high school, the coach moved me to the defensive line and I excelled. I tried to do the same in the classroom.

After one season at the junior college – two if you count the one before the war – I transferred to Stephen F. Austin University, a Nacogdoches school located a few hundred miles north of Beaumont. There, I played football for two years, earned the captain's armband and played well again on the defensive line. I lettered in football, baseball and track, competed in rodeos on the weekend, worked two jobs and maintained my grades. I focused on history, agriculture, geography and animal husbandry, the study of breeding and caring for farm animals.

In 1948, Helen gave birth to our second child, Susan. A year later, I earned my degree in education. With a growing family and a desire to put my college education to use in the workforce, I planned for possible careers ahead. Then, I received a phone call from out of the blue.

Some people think they were born to be coaches, and I'm sure many are. Me? I just kind of fell into it in the strangest of ways.

BUM LESSON: Recognize signs from God.

As a young man, I wasn't purposely stubborn-headed when it came to the Lord. I simply didn't know better. I thought if I did the right thing – chose the right paths for my life – I'd go to heaven. Luckily, He didn't hold that against me. God pulled some obvious strings in my life for many years to come.

The Bible talks a lot about paths. If you're like me, the path I want to remain on is the one that takes me to heaven. I didn't know until later in life the only way down God's path is through His only son, Jesus Christ.

If you're struggling in life to find your own path, there's something you can do right now to help quickly locate it. Stop reading, close your eyes and believe with all your heart Jesus Christ is the way to God. Say, "I accept Jesus Christ as my Savior."

If you acknowledge Him, He will undoubtedly prompt you to take a promising left turn even when all you've ever known is to veer right.

CHAPTER 5

THE WORKMAN'S WAY

"Work hard and become a leader; be lazy and never succeed." – Proverbs 12:24

Y ou might not care to read this book had I not been a head coach in the NFL for so long. Of course, I didn't just show up one day to coach the Houston Oilers. I worked my way up the football ranks for decades as a player, high school coach, college coach and NFL assistant. In the process, I learned a great deal about becoming a sound leader.

Before I developed my philosophy for coaching, I rekindled a relationship I developed with Elbert Pickell, my former high school coach in Beaumont. After I graduated from Stephen F. Austin University, Pickell called me from Nederland and offered me an assistant coaching job. To be honest, I didn't really want the job. At the time, I didn't think I'd make a career out of coaching.

I agreed, however, and in 1950 I moved my family to Nederland, a small community south of Beaumont. I entered coaching during a unique period in the sport's history.

Texas high school football emerged during the twentieth century as an institution in and of itself. Football became like the oil and cattle industries, and almost more important. The men who served as coaches largely approached their jobs with sensibilities they gathered during the Great Depression, World War II and life back on the ranch (1). Those coaches in turn shaped the sport, branded it with its image and steered it like a herd to market. We also molded an entire generation of young men.

"The game at its peak began in the era after the victory in World War II and ended sometime during the late 1960s," wrote Ty Cashion in his book Pigskin Pulpit (2). "The coaches whose careers began around the time of World War II and continued through the tumultuous social changes in the decades that followed possessed a conviction that football imparted the qualities that would turn fuzzy-chinned boys into stalwart young men. The majority of coaches hailed from humble, and in many cases destitute, environments. Typically they possessed a rural southernness. They also shared a sense of athleticism and became accustomed to the military regimen that characterized their youth."

In time, I imparted my life's lessons and helped to shape the sport not only in Texas high schools, but in the way it's played in the professional ranks today. My first year on the sideline offered little hint of this, however. In 1950, assistant coaches, at least in Texas, were a luxury. Until this period, most teams had one coach – the head coach. The sport began to grow, though, in part from an improved highway system, fleets of high school buses that allowed distant teams to compete and new stadiums. As a result, schools began increasing their football budgets. Just as those who returned from war rebuilt the country, schools rebuilt their sports programs, and football was a priority. Assistant coaches, however, were not.

I didn't like assistant coaching because I didn't get to do anything during practice. Coach Pickell did everything. I stood around with my arms crossed most of the time.

Never having had an assistant coach before, Pickell didn't know how to incorporate me. Still, I vowed to learn the job. I studied Pickell, his mannerisms, schemes and approach to player interactions. A year later, Pickell left for another coaching job. Nederland suddenly needed a new head coach.

After a full season of idle time on the sideline – and working as a roughneck in the oil fields during the summer – a head coaching job presented itself to me for the first time. Of course, being young and ignorant, I applied for the job and got it. They offered me $2,700 a year.

"No. I won't work for that," I said. "But I will work for $2,750 a year."

I really held out on them. Joking aside, I needed more money, and I could have earned considerably more in the oil fields. I had no idea I'd end up loving coaching, being the boss. It just hit me, and once it did, football became my life until the day I walked off the field.

In Nederland, I inherited a losing program and admit I wasn't a good coach at first. Shoot, I thought I knew everything. A friend and I traveled to Rice University to watch spring training, and we'd sit in the stands and second-guess the coaches. I didn't know what I was doing, but I sure acted like I did.

Maybe it was my naivety or my healthy dose of confidence, but I began to incorporate tactics into football that helped to revolutionize the sport, and I'm proud to say so. I hired two assistant coaches: Emmett McKenzie, a science teacher who'd never played a down of football in his life, and Vernon Ramke. Together, we visited college practices any chance we got. I personally sat in the stands every Thursday for three years while Paul "Bear" Bryant, the legendary college coach, held practices at Texas A&M University. I studied how to coach the different positions, filmed my practices and dissected player mistakes, as well as the means to correct them. During the off season when most coaches left for other jobs, my assistants and I studied football. I started thinking about the game the minute the season was over. Who did I improve the most during the first years? Myself.

From the lessons I learned while studying college practices, I implemented and devised new methods for holding my own. First, I put my assistant coaches to work. If you have three coaches, one guy can teach the offensive linemen, one guy can coach the running backs and so on. You get so much more done. Secondly, I divided my team into player sets and drilled them independently, a move thought to be the first of its kind in Texas high school football history. Each position had a station, and each player received detailed instructions about techniques, schemes and execution.

I meticulously planned practices and posted the day's schedule for players to view. Because I squeezed as much coaching as I could into the allotted time, players sprinted from drill to drill and often went without water breaks. They didn't have time to slow down. I'm not afraid to say I was way ahead of most high school coaches, and my players had better fundamental techniques because of it. I've always thought if we run 30 plays during practice and you run 20 plays, we're going to be better than you over the span of a season.

Herb Adkins became one of the many boys who played for me in high school who then went on to succeed in college and at life.

"Yeah, he screwed me up," Adkins said, laughed and then paused. "… In a good way. We had drills that were so organized that we knew what we were going to do every second of that entire day, from calisthenics to techniques. He had it up on the board. When he blew that whistle, you better run. There was no walking between drills. After every game, he did an amazing thing: He graded us on every play. We either got a plus or a minus. Then, he added them up. If you played good, you got a B or an A. You could get a D, too, though. You didn't want your buddy outscoring you, so you gave more effort. I wasn't the greatest student, but I sure did OK in football. When I went to Baylor, I knew more about football and my position than any of those coaches did. Bum was more organized in technique than any other coach I ever had."

For our hard work, we enjoyed great success at Nederland, which had a long track record of losing. From 1951 to 1956, we amassed a 58-11 record and made the playoffs five of six seasons. I never thought much about records. I define success by how much you improve a kid from the beginning to the end of the year. The attractive thing to me about football was getting kids to improve. That feeling continued until the day I quit coaching.

Neal Morgan played for me at Nederland. He said he immediately noticed a difference between me and any coach he'd ever played for.

"He stepped right in and taught us stuff nobody ever taught us. He also wouldn't lie to you. Hell, we believed everything he told us," Morgan said. "When I saw him for the first time, I was sitting in the field house. My friend, Charles Thomas, said, 'Man, you see that? When he walked in, something walked in in front of him.' He already had that aura. Coach Pickell was good as he could be, but he didn't know football like Bum did."

After high school, Morgan attended Wharton Junior College. The school accepted him based, in part, on my recommendation. He became a starter and a captain, and blossomed with a college education. One day, the school's dean plucked Morgan from the hallway during a class break.

"Scared the hell out of me," Morgan said. "The dean told me: 'I just want to congratulate you. You are the first football player in the history of this school who got all A's in English.' Coach Phillips taught us football fundamentals, but he also taught us how to better ourselves in life."

Morgan went on to author several books. He also gave my son, Wade, his first coaching job.

Part of the reason players at all levels listened to me is after a lot of hard work I finally knew what I was talking about. As my mentor Paul "Bear" Bryant always said: "It's not the will to win that matters. It's the will to prepare to win that matters." We prepared to win, and so we did.

In addition to studying college practices, I began attending dozens of coaching clinics, which brought together the best football minds from around the state and country. We gathered during the days in classrooms and on the fields. We studied the sport, its innovations and truisms. Most coaches who regularly attended the clinics ended up in my room for late-night brainstorming sessions. I dispelled wisdom as well as absorbed it. Bob Barfield remembers as many as 40 and 50 coaches on occasion packed into my room to exchange ideas (3). Hugh Hamm, then a young assistant coach at Carrolton Turner, recalled asking me a question and "next thing I knew he was handing me the chalk and wanted to know what I thought."

Even legendary college coaches – Darrell Royal, Frank Broyles and Bear Bryant – joined the crowd. Contrary to public opinion, Bryant never screamed and hollered, and I tried to imitate him. He was not an X's and O's guy. He was a people guy. He could take players and get them to do it better than anyone I ever saw. He just had a knack for getting people to play better. His talks were never about running off tackle. His talks were about *who* is running off tackle.

Toward the end of my coaching stint at Nederland, Coach Bryant and I became close friends. In 1956, the year before I left Nederland to coach in the college ranks, Bear asked me to devise a simple system to call defensive plays, and I went to work creating it. For years, Bryant had wanted a way to call playing techniques, but he'd yet to concoct a system. I figured it out and went up there and told him about it. Commentators talk about it still on TV, only most don't know what they're talking about or where it came from. You might hear NFL analysts these days comment when a player uses the "5 technique" or the "2 technique." Well, that's my baby, and I gave birth to it as a high school coach five decades ago. Bryant, meanwhile, installed the system in his program, too.

Joe Sibley played defense under me at Nederland. He remembers the system this way: "It simplified things for players," Sibley said. "We spent less time thinking about what to do and more time doing it." Basically, the system used numbers to alert players about which offensive gap to cover and where to line up on the opposing lineman or in the defensive backfield. The idea was to cover all lanes and to make assignments simple to digest for players on the move. The numbers technique tells you not only where to line up, but how to play. It gave gap responsibility, where as before it was "get the ball carrier" responsibility. It made defense easy to call, easy to run and easy to learn.

Another coaching nuance I learned early on is the ability to build a system around talent, or lack thereof. If, for example, my crop included a solid quarterback, the offensive scheme leaned heavily on the passing game. The next year, we might lean on the running game and the defense. You took what you had, identified it and then created a system that worked with your players' strengths. I never fell for thinking the system would win for you. We did things the players were good at – not what I wanted them to be good at.

While my organization and player development techniques helped my team to prepare for success, there's another trait I possess players like most to talk about. Critics in the pros criticized me for being a player's coach, but I wouldn't have any other label. To me, a player's coach works a kid hard, gives him a pat on the back or a kick in the rear when needed. I always invested time in a player because underneath his helmet stood a person with needs, goals and wants. Plays aren't nearly as important as the players running them.

At Nederland, our team name was the Bulldogs and our mascot was fitting. We weren't talented or pretty – we were rough and tough. Throughout my career, I worked hard to prod underdogs into top dogs. To succeed as a coach, I had to make mediocre players average, average players good and good players great. Look at the roster of any of my teams in high school, college and the NFL. They were only sprinkled with stars, yet we were able to turn those players and teams into winners. God blessed me with common sense and the talent to lead. He taught me how to get the best out of people. I learned to be firm with a kid, to be honest, critical without being nasty – and you don't treat them all the same. You know you've succeeded when a player loves football so much they'll do anything to play, and when they need the sport more than it needs them.

"He just had a rapport with players like no other coach I'd ever seen," Morgan said. "He really cared what happened to you or how you did. That just came across. It still does."

Adkins was a relatively thin high school player who fought in the trenches of the offensive line. These days he lives in Shiner, Texas.

"You just loved Bum. He treated everybody fair," Adkins said. "He was more like a dad to you in many ways. He wanted us to do right. He wanted us to get our school work done and be a good citizen. If you wasn't, you weren't going to play."

By all measures, Adkins shouldn't have been a good football player. He lacked star talent and the size in a position marked by bulky teens. During one game, he struggled to block an opponent. Adkins remembers losing the fight on almost every down. During a break, he ran to the sideline and told me he couldn't get the job done.

"Don't you ever say you can't," I told him. "Say you can't hardly."

"I didn't have a lot of ability, but after that talk I had a lot of want to," Adkins said. "We weren't the best athletes, but he made us. I went on to play college football for Baylor. I played against the greats in college – Merlin Olsen, Bob Lilly – and I held my own. I'd whip your butt no matter who you were. He instilled a lot of that in me. I got my law degree at Baylor. Later, I built and sold an oil company, bought a farm and retired to work cattle. I owe it all to Bum. He was the influence all the way around. I know how coaches should be, and they should be more like Bum Phillips."

My favorite high school memory of a player who overcame hardship is the story of Joe Sibley. Sibley was born with clubfoot, a deformity in newborns that forces a baby's foot to point down and inward. When he was a child, doctors tried to straighten the foot by twisting it and setting it in a cast. The treatment didn't work, and he wore braces on his legs. One day his mother held him in her arms while sitting in the hallway of a Louisiana hospital.

"As luck would have it," Sibley said, "the good Lord came into my life that day."

A doctor walked by Sibley and his mother. He stopped, turned and said, "Ma'am, would you mind taking the shoe off that boy's foot?"

"Sure," the mother replied.

The doctor examined Sibley's foot. "My gosh. Who has been butchering on this boy? Well, I work at Shriners Hospital in Shreveport. Can you have this boy up at 9 in the morning? I want to have a look at it."

Sibley stayed in the Shreveport hospital for several months. He underwent numerous surgeries. Because of his deformity, an inch-and-a-half difference grew between his good leg and bad. To compensate, doctors stunted the growth in his good leg. Around the time of his sixteenth birthday – having undergone several other surgeries and endured ongoing treatment – the doctor measured his legs.

"Well," the doctor said, "they're both the same length. That's all we can do for you."

"Can I play football?" Sibley asked.

"You can do anything you want," the doctor said.

While Sibley played sandlot football as a boy, his mother had always refused to allow him to join an organized team. She was so strongly against the idea she once chased him with a wood 2-by-4 and threw it at him in anger.

Once doctors said his lower body could safely carry his weight at a gallop, she changed her mind. Even so, he remained scarred with the physical reminder he wasn't like most boys.

"My bad leg is very small compared to the good one. Doctors clipped the tendons to muscles in the calf," Sibley said. "All I have is an up and down motion – no lateral movement like with the elbow. Because of this, I had poor balance but I just wanted to play. Football was the big thing in Nederland. All the dads worked out at the refineries together and they'd start betting a month's salary on a damn high school football game, even when they couldn't afford it."

In the span of a few weeks, Sibley suffered a string of injuries. First, he broke his nose covering a kickoff. The helmets didn't include facemasks then, and he wound up on the wrong side of a nasty collision. Two games later, he broke his finger. The bone split into a compound fracture. The injury I remember most, however, is the one he suffered a game later.

Sibley tried to block a large defender while his running back sped in behind him on an outside trap. As would-be tacklers and teammates swarmed him from all sides, Sibley was hit on his left knee, which was his good leg. The collision tore his medial collateral ligament, and he felt the pain of bone rubbing on bone. He insisted on playing the remainder of the game, though. He had tape on his broken nose, tape over the fracture on his finger and the worrisome limp of a teen who ought not to be walking.

Despite the pain, Sibley refused to leave the game. I can remember him limping down the field. Oh, man, was he tough. On top of it, he worked his entire high school career at nights for a funeral home. He was a special kind of guy.

After the game ended, we dropped Sibley off at the funeral home so he could work. The next day, I received a call from a doctor who treated the teen for his injuries.

"We're going to have to put a cast on," the doc said.

I agreed with the doctor, and Sibley cried like a baby. He didn't want a cast, which would keep him off the football field.

"If I can take it, you all ought to be able to take it, too," he told us.

Now you know how much he loved football. He went on to coach for me in Nederland and Jacksonville, Texas. We grew close and remain so today. Sibley is 75 years old now and lives in California.

"We might be men now but Bum was and is always like my Daddy," Sibley said.

I coached across the state during the 1950s and 1960s – Nederland, Jacksonville, Amarillo and Port Neches-Groves. What I loved most about high school football is that it's about today. It's not about tomorrow. This is why Sibley didn't want to put his leg in the cast. In high school, kids are anxious to learn what you have to teach them, and they play like it's the last time they're going to play. Once they get into college, they start thinking about playing pro ball. When they get to pro ball, they start thinking about making money.

Like any coach – at any level – people expected me to win. In its own way, the pressure was no less at Nederland High School, where I started out, than it was at New Orleans, where I finished my NFL career (4). Yet only in the high school ranks did I truly feel pressure from the community to juggle the demands of winning with the equal responsibility of keeping sight of the kids who played the game. It's the high school coach who is in the toughest spot, and I don't think most people stop to think about it. I learned how to be a professional coach when I coached in high school and it's still my favorite place to have coached.

After a 50-plus-year football career, I had plenty of successes and two regrets, one of which is a failure on my part to teach players about God. If I knew more about God then, I could have talked a lot about Him. The more you study the Bible, the more you go to church, the more you're around church people, the more you think about what's coming rather than what has been. If you're thinking in terms of what's going to happen, you won't make some of the mistakes you make now.

In the end, football sure ain't about winning and losing. I'd rather have influenced some kids right in a more Godly way. I knew the kids looked up at me as a coach and I could have used my influence a lot more than I did. If you can make a guy think about things, you can change him over time. There's a reward for learning about God and making Jesus the center of your life. It's called heaven.

Before I discuss my next biggest coaching regret, I ought to admit some other high school coaching mistakes of a lesser degree. For instance, I cussed, worked players on Sunday and often refused water breaks. This was common at the time, but I know better now.

My next regret is what I did to Jack Sanford. I believe wholeheartedly a man must keep his word, and I taught this principle to my players. During my second year at Nederland, I bumped into a wild-looking, athletic student who didn't play football. He was the kind of kid who even at first glance appeared to be a natural at sports, the kind who can run headfirst into a wedge of defenders and somehow slink out the other side. Sanford just looked like a football player.

I asked him to tryout for the team. He agreed and earned all-district and second team all-state honors his junior year. He was on his way to a college career.

"Coach Phillips told me: 'All you have to do is go make a touchdown, come right back here and sit beside me,'" Sanford said 60 years later. "That's what he told me."

Given his high school success, Sanford developed a dream to play professional football. To stay in shape during the off-season, he joined the track team. I told my free-spirited junior the same rules we apply to football apply to track, as well.

"If you go out for track, you have to stick with it," I told him. "You can't miss practice."

One day, Sanford missed practice. The track coach alerted me and I reminded the speedster if he missed more practices he couldn't play football. Well, he missed another practice. And then another. The track coach finally kicked him off the team.

The next year, Sanford strolled into the first day of football spring training. He expected me to hand him his jersey as I did the year before.

"Nope," I said. "You can't have it. Your word is not good."

Without football and the chance to play in college and possibly the pros, Sanford quit school and joined the Navy.

"It broke my heart," Sanford said. "I had my heart set on the NFL, being like those heroes: Slinging Sammy Baugh. I was just a dumb kid who didn't feel like rules applied to him, I guess. Coach nipped it in the bud. It gave me a whole different perspective on life. It actually helped me. I stayed in that little town after the Navy, got married and raised four children. After school, I got into the electrical game. I became a supervisor, made good money for the time. I retired from the International Brotherhood of Electrical Workers 479. I wound up twisting wires instead of catching footballs."

While Sanford said he almost immediately understood the reasoning behind my decision, I never forgave myself. My threat was meant to scare him straight, not to end a young man's career. That mistake stuck with me forever. I was stupid, and I felt horrible for it. I thought I understood the full meaning of keeping your word, but you have to allow for a person to err. I proved a point at someone else's expense, and I don't mind admitting I'm wrong.

In January 2010, I called Sanford. I heard he'd just gotten out of the hospital and was staying at his daughter's home in Nederland. Sanford was 74 years old when we talked for the first time in six decades. He'd recently suffered a stroke. A year before the stroke, he hurt his neck in a car wreck. Then, he got bull-headed and tried to shake his blue jeans off his legs. He lost his balance, fell and hurt his neck again.

After doctors released him from the hospital, his Nederland daughter took him to her house. He planned on staying there a few days to recoup before traveling with his son to Houston.

"Then, the phone rang," Sanford said. "Before I could answer it, it went dead. So, I just pushed recall and it started dialing. Hell, I didn't know who'd called."

The phone at my house rang. Sanford listened intently into the ear piece.

"Jack," I said.

"Yes, sir," Sanford said.

"This is Bum Phillips."

"I could have fallen over," Sanford said. "A celebrity calling a washed up old guy like me? That made me feel so great. I sure appreciate the time I played for him. He was so smart at football and life in general. I told him he raised a good son. I watch Wade on TV and you can just tell he's good. When Coach Bum Phillips called me and said that what he did had bothered him this whole while, I tried to emphasize, 'Coach, don't feel that way. In this country, we've got laws and rules. I didn't live up to them rules. You did what was necessary, and by doing that, you made me grow up. Heck, I forgive you. I'm just happy to hear from you.'"

The brief phone conversation helped me to make amends for a regret that weighed heavily on me for 60 years. I feel better now, but I'll never forget it. Don't ever hold a grudge against a kid. They're going to screw up. If he screws up, correct him right then and there and leave it on the field.

BUM LESSON: Do what you love.

I can't stress this lesson enough. We spend so much of our time, energy and thoughts on our profession that you do yourself a great disservice if you fail to find a career you love. I can speak from experience. I loved football so much I can honestly say I never worked a day for 50 years. Football was my passion. I loved everything about it and money didn't make a difference. I'd have coached no matter what they paid, and you'll do a better job if it never seems like work.

What are you passionate about? What if you could do what you enjoy for a paycheck? I'm not suggesting you quit your job today to become a professional golfer, but I am saying you ought to give more thought to enjoyable work.

God plants talents and passions in us all, and it's our job to follow those gifts. When we do what we love, and we do the job well, we not only honor God, but we become fulfilled.

Ecclesiastes 2:24 says it better than I can: "Nothing is better for a man than that he should eat and drink, and that his soul should enjoy good in his labor."

CHAPTER 6

THE COLLEGE WAY

"No one can serve two masters. For you will hate one and love the other; you will be devoted to one and despise the other." – Matthew 6:24

Y ou pay a price to become a winning football coach, and one of the prices I paid was time away from family. I never missed one day of work during my entire coaching career. My absence from home, which proved fruitful on the field, created a rift between me, my first wife and six children. I loved my family. We just barely saw one another.

I was taught from an early age if you take a job, any job, you do it well. When it came to football, I loved the game so much I often worked until 3 or 4 in the morning, on weekends and through holidays. We still don't make a big deal about birthdays and Thanksgiving. Because I coached in so many different cities, to this day my kids' birthplaces are linked to a town, a time and a team.

There's a lot to be said about hard work, providing and setting a good example for children. You can't become a good person without sacrifice. It's another thing to sacrifice your family, especially for long periods, in an effort to provide and become a good person. If I could do it again, I'd work just as hard at football but also at being more present for my children. Please remember, I grew up during a different era – during a time when men did little else but work. I have enough good sense now to know the wisdom in finding a more Godly balance.

Even so, I still believe you owe it to yourself, your family and God to better yourself. If you accept a job, even if you don't like it, perform the work to the best of your ability. Too many people cut themselves short and fail to move upward in life.

I cut myself short once. Fellow coaches during my early days on the sideline tried to get me to devote my life to God. I scoffed at the idea then, and it haunted me for decades.

I coached high school football in Nederland until I was 34. By 1957, after six years, I'd earned respect and my stripes. I graduated to college coaching the day Paul "Bear" Bryant offered me a job at Texas A&M University. I jumped at the chance.

Bear Bryant was one of the most famous coaches of all time – still is, even though he died in 1983. As a teen, he earned his nickname by wrestling a captive bear during a show near his hometown. We got along because we share a great many similarities. We were born 10 years apart and in rural areas. We both rode wagons to town as children. We were both raucous kids and determined from an early age. And, of course, most people know us by a lasting, one-syllable nickname.

I've met and dined with U.S. presidents, movie stars and musicians, but Bear Bryant was the most captivating, impressive person I ever met. He could walk into a room and everyone sat up. He'd sit there and not say a word. He'd fiddle with a pocket on the front of his dress coat, pull out a cigarette, light up and lean back. First he'd tell all his assistant coaches what we were doing well. Then, he'd offer suggestions in a calm voice.

"Well, maybe you ought to think about this or that," he'd say.

Bear Bryant had by far the biggest influence on my life. He just had a way with people. He could pull the talent out of a person like a magician does with those never-ending, colorful scarves. He had a way of explaining things without having to curse and, contrary to popular belief, he didn't holler and scream. He never had to say, "Let me have your attention." He would brag on people, make you feel like you were the most important person in the world to him.

In the late 1970s, they wrote a book about me called, "He Ain't No Bum." Bear Bryant wrote the book's foreword. I don't include his words here to brag, but I'd be lying to you if I said they don't make me proud.

"When (Bum) first came to me, the players already respected him because he had a high school coaching record of 90-something and 2 at Nederland, Texas," Bryant wrote (1). "Bum has a great knack for handling people. If people think he's corny, well, then I'm corny. Bum's a terrific individual with a lot of class. He's got a great football mind. He's a hard worker. I've been knowing him for many years, at least 30, and I have never heard anyone say anything about Bum Phillips that wasn't complimentary."

When I first read Bryant's words decades ago, I felt good and then I laughed. Coach Bryant had never called me Bum like he did for the book's foreword. He always called me "Bun." I think he refused to call me by my nickname partly because he had a subtle sense of humor and partly because he saw how hard I worked. He'd seen me in the stands at his practices every Thursday for three years, and he sat in my hotel room when groups talked football during all those coaching clinics. I bet he felt calling me "Bum" resonated with unfair connotations.

At Texas A&M University, I was the low man on the totem pole. When Bryant announced after my first year that he was leaving to take the University of Alabama head coaching job, I had a few options. I could return to high school coaching, apply for the Texas A&M top job or follow Bryant to Alabama, but I didn't want to leave Texas. It didn't make sense for me to leave and begin work in a new retirement system because I had seven years in the Texas system. One night, I rode in an elevator with Bear Bryant during a break from the Gator Bowl. He used our short trip to a top-level restaurant to pass along some advice.

"You ain't going to get the A&M head coaching job," Bryant said.

"I didn't apply for it," I told him.

"I know, but all the players went to the university's board of regents and said they wanted you to be the new head coach," he said. "When they went up and talked to the board of regents, they killed your chances right there. Boards of regents don't listen to players. Why don't you come with me to Alabama?"

"I don't want to leave Texas," I said. "I think I'll go back and coach high school."

"Bun, now I don't want you to make a mistake," Bryant told me. "Don't take a job just to get a check. I'm going to keep you on my payroll until you get the right job. If you take the wrong job, they're going to forget about all those wins. In football, all they remember is the last year. Take your time. I tell you what, Bun, make sure wherever you go, they have a good chance to win. You got to win. The only way you'll go to the next level is if you go to a winning program."

Bryant was willing to take money out of his own pocket and pay me until I found the right job. I wanted to make my own money, though. I thought it would be better for a feller to be working if he could work.

About a week later, I got a call from the high school in Jacksonville, Texas. They hadn't won a game there in three years. If I'd listened to Bryant, I would have turned down the offer. Well, I have a soft spot for underdogs and challenges. I accepted the job immediately.

By the time we moved in 1958 to Jacksonville, Texas, my fourth child, Dee Jean, was born. When I accepted the Amarillo coaching job in 1959, Andrea was born. In 1962, we moved again, this time to Texas Western University, which is today known as the University of Texas at El Paso. My son, Wade, still jokes that any time all of us were in a car together, the kids feared we were moving.

At El Paso, I met a former player who takes credit in jest for praying me into a relationship with Jesus Christ. John Paul Young and I met at the school and we also later coached together in the pros at Houston and New Orleans. At the time, Young had played for four years and became a student assistant coach.

"I still pray for his and hissuns every day," Young said. "I thank the Lord for his witness and his ministry. Bum always had a lot of good Christian guys around him. He's always had a lot of Christian principles in him, which he taught us. People think about Bum as the John Wayne of NFL football. I just hope people don't forget what a great man and coach he is. He's got to be in the top two or three, character-wise, who has ever come down the pike."

You can't be around guys like Young and not want them to succeed. You can't be around guys like Bear Bryant and not learn about generosity. One day, Young called me all excited. He said he was getting married to one of the school's cheerleaders. A day or so passed, and I called for Young to come into my office. It was early afternoon and, of course, I ribbed him a bit. The coaching staff and I had collected some money, $10 apiece. I handed him the envelope filled with cash and then told him he might need the money as a married man.

"This brings tears to my eyes every time I tell the story," Young said, taking a breath. "Golly, I appreciated it, you know. We all hugged and they teased me some more, and then Coach Phillips said he'd walk me to my car."

I remember that walk – out of the stadium and into the parking lot. When we got to his car, I asked Young for his keys. He had an old, ugly, black 1954 car. So, I pointed to my brand new blue and white Chrysler New Yorker and told him to sit in the driver's seat. The university gave me the car, so he thought I wanted him to take it to wash it. Instead, I told him he was going to drive the New Yorker on his honeymoon, that I'd see him at his wedding and I'd better see him for next year's spring training.

"Then, Coach Phillips pitched another envelope on my lap and said, 'Get out of here.' When he left, I checked the tank and it was full of gas. I looked into the envelope. I'm telling you there were five $100 bills and a gas card in there," Young said, pausing to stop a cry. "That's something, isn't it? That was a lot of money in the 1950s – still is. You see now why I'd do just about anything for that man? What that meant to me and my wife is very special."

While Young prayed in private for me to find a relationship with Christ, he wasn't the only peer during this time who pushed me toward the Almighty. Chief Wilson, one of my assistant coaches along the way, tried like mad to get me to become spiritual, but I just wouldn't. As far as I was concerned, I didn't want to talk about it. The last time he brought it up, I told him to stop that talk. He got up and left, quit football and entered the ministry. I didn't see him again for 10 years.

"It was important to me that Bum found God," Wilson said. "I just thought that it would be a shame if such a good man didn't go to heaven because he was too stubborn to listen to what I and others had to say. But that was Bum. He did things his way."

One day years later and after I retired, I sat at a table and signed autographs for fans. So many people stopped I lost track of faces and time. I'd ask each person who they wanted me to sign my notes to. Then, I looked up and saw Chief Wilson standing there at the front of the long line. He'd stood in the line until it was his turn, and I immediately stopped signing autographs, pulled him to the side and hugged him. We talked and agreed to keep in touch. Since our visit, he spent time with me on my Goliad ranch, and we never lost touch again.

Like I've said, you bounce around quite a bit as a coach. During the years, I've been offered chances to stay put, jobs I could have held for life. At Port Neches in 1963, the superintendent said I could coach one year, 10 years or for as long as I wanted. When I wanted to quit football, he said he'd give me an administrative job. Two years later, though, I was offered a job at the University of Houston. The athletic director for the university led me into the Astrodome where the team played. I walked up a ramp, onto this beautiful mezzanine and I was instantly floored. I'd never seen a dome in all my life, and at first glance I knew it would be a great recruiting tool. I was sold right there. The field, however, was solid dirt by the time the football team got to practicing on it. The Houston Astros tore it up. We had to line the dirt and paint it green because the first game was nationally televised.

It looked great on TV, but it was as hard as the devil. It wasn't until the next year they topped the dirt with Astroturf.

In 1967, I landed my first job in the NFL as a defensive line coach with the San Diego Chargers. I'd made it to the NFL thanks to hard work, recommendations from the nation's top college coaches and a phone interview with Sid Gillman, the team's head coach. I'd never met the man but he hired me sight unseen.

When Gillman hired me, I suddenly needed to sell my Houston-area home and find a new one in San Diego. One day, my daughter Cicely and I were in our home all alone. Cicely, who was in the eighth grade, sat in the living room and we talked. Then, the phone rang. I picked it up and a man on the other end asked questions about our floor plan, the area and the neighbors. We hadn't even put the house on the market yet, so I was a bit confused. Well, he said he needed to move right away, had seven children and spent most weekends and nights at work. Because of this, he wanted a one-story home in a good neighborhood and quality school district – traits I'd looked for when moving in years before.

The similarities between us, and the way our home fit his wishes perfectly, made me curious.

"What do you do?" I asked.

"I'm a football coach," he said. "I'm coming to Houston to coach for the Oilers."

"Is that right?" I said. "I'm a coach and I'm headed to San Diego to work for the Chargers."

Needless to say, we hit it off and he agreed over the phone to buy our house. I hung up the phone and turned to Cicely.

"Dad yelled, 'I just sold the house over the phone!'" Cicely said. "He was just so tickled. I'll never forget how happy it made him."

Many years later, when Cicely was a young woman, she met a man while dining inside a Houston restaurant.

Attracted to each other, they talked excitedly for some time. They discussed their lives, upbringing and frequent moves as children – everything but their football coaches for fathers.

After awhile, the man said, "You're Bum Phillips' daughter, aren't you?"

"Why would you say something like that?" Cicely said, protective of telling near-strangers her dad coached in the NFL.

As it turns out, the man Cicely met in the Houston restaurant was the son of Hugh Devore, the coach who bought our house during the late 1960s. Devore was recruited as a player by Notre Dame's Knute Rockne and he later coached for the Oilers and Green Bay Packers.

As for Cicely and Devore's son, the two left the restaurant together and later married and had seven children.

My first wife delivered my sixth and last child, Kimann, on the day of the 1967 NFL draft. When I arrived in San Diego, Gillman spotted me in the airport only because I was the lone guy in the crowd to wear a cowboy hat and boots. Gillman was the only one who wore a bowtie and suit. It was quite a shock for both of us, I'm sure.

My stay in San Diego was short-lived, though. By 1972, I left the NFL and returned to college to coach at Southern Methodist University in Dallas. Gillman had turned in his resignation, and when he did he resigned for everyone.

At SMU, as in many stops, I befriended coaches who became pals for life. Head coach Hayden Fry brought Andy Everest and I to the school, and we lived under the stadium while our families remained at home to finish the school year. Everest and I slept in a bathroom-turned-modest-bedroom. We had two iron beds and a dresser, and we could hear the lawnmowers cut blades on the practice fields.

"Bum and I are as close as friends as he probably has and I honor that," Everest, who also coached with me at the New Orleans Saints, said. "There's not a phony bone in his body."

Our families have traveled together – to the Grand Canyon, Yellowstone and Big Bend national parks – in a big bus I bought after retiring to my Goliad ranch.

"One day, we got down to Sanderson, Texas," Everest said. "We pulled into this old filling station. This guy came running out to fill some gas for us. He looked at Bum and then came running over to me. 'Is that Bum Phillips?' he said. He ran inside and jumped on the phone. Before we knew it, about 25 people showed up. When they did, I joked, 'Yeah, do you know who I am? I'm Paul Newman.' Even when we went into Mexico, people came running up when they saw Bum."

Everest and I probably wouldn't have become friends had it not been for Hayden Fry. Like Bear Bryant, Fry was a legendary college coach. When Gillman resigned from San Diego, Fry called me about becoming the defensive coordinator for SMU.

Both Fry and I grew up country, like the rodeo, served in the military, befriended U.S. presidents and love football. We were like brothers.

"I was inducted into the College Football Hall of Fame," Fry said. "During the ceremony, they showed a documentary. It started with a letter Coach Phillips wrote about me and then included a talk from President George Bush."

Fry watched my children grow and my son morph into a great football mind. He makes sure to watch every Dallas Cowboys game now, and he'll call if he spots me in a stadium suite watching a game live. Fry also coached at Arkansas when a guy named Barry Switzer roomed with Jerry Jones.

One day at SMU, Fry and I watched film on Ohio State University, an upcoming opponent. It was clear we were going to struggle to move the ball on offense, so I suggested we install a fake punt, and we called it the Bumarooski. The play called for the center to snap the ball to the fullback – who would fake a handoff to the up-back – and for the punter to act like he punted. The fullback would stand nonchalantly with the ball while everyone else ran around. After a few seconds, the fullback would then dart off for a first down. The play worked against OSU and turned out to be the first of its kind.

"Bum is a genius, and I don't just mean on the offensive and defensive sides of the ball," Fry said. "One of the smartest football coaches there ever was. He was way ahead of his time. I think you have to know Bum to understand how sincere, honest and straightforward he is. He's a complete man, very sensitive but very tough. You combine those things, you have a great person. I paid him more at SMU as a defensive coordinator than I made as head coach and athletic director."

Like I said at the beginning of this chapter, you pay a price to become a winning football coach, and one of the prices I paid was time away from family. Football offered me great friendships, insight and memories, but the sport took from my children. As I told these college-era stories, my daughter Dee Jean sat nearby on the couch in my Goliad home. She wore a Dallas Cowboys jersey in honor of her brother. I love my children, and I have a strong relationship with them now. But when I coached, almost all of my attention and affection were on my other kids – players and assistant coaches.

Dee Jean used to visit me when we held the Houston Oilers' training camp at Sam Houston State University – where she was a student – and she watched me with the team. She didn't realize it until years later, but she became jealous of the players. I always coached, walked up and down sidelines or spent time outside football with the staff and players.

"Why would Dad tell the players he loved them, but not tell me the same?" Dee Jean said. "I remember Dad talking to me and Andrea when we were in high school. He sat down and said a few words. We tried to express ourselves but we began to cry. We didn't know how to talk to him and I don't think he knew how to talk to us. It was awkward all of the time. We had to think of things to ask him, so we mainly asked him about football because we knew that was his love."

Dee Jean, now an adult, almost cried when she discussed her childhood, and I leaned in from my chair at the table and told her I love her.

"Well," I said, "I hope you know I always loved you. If I didn't, I'd have cut you from the family like I cut the players from the team."

She laughed.

Truth is I just wasn't around when my children were younger. While the girls struggled to find ways to relate, Wade used a clever trick to spend time with me.

"When I was growing up, Daddy didn't come home until I was asleep," Wade said. "So, even when I was a little kid, I'd hang around the field house where he was working. I became water boy for his high school team. Later on when I was in high school, I just stayed after school and hung around the coach's office. Even during my freshman year at college, I was on the phones during ball games with the coaches in the stands. He's always going to be a hero to me – not just a dad, but a hero."

Before I learned what it means to show real love to my children, my football career in the mid 1970s propelled me for good to the NFL. I still get goose bumps when I think about what happened professionally when I returned to Houston to coach the Oilers. Without the fan-fueled hysteria that swirled around our team, I might not be writing this book right now. Likewise, I might never have met the football player who eventually led me to God. I can thank the Houston Oilers for many things, but as you'll soon learn, the team spurred for me a lifetime of happy memories, a strong relationship with Christ and an open heart from which I now show love to the children who craved it for so long.

BUM LESSON: Tips for becoming an effective leader.

I've learned quite a bit about winning and losing, winners and losers. After I retired from football, big companies hired me to speak to their employees, who were often upper-management types. During the years, I found a proven system for finding quality people and for weeding out those you should avoid. While you can write a book about choosing great company, the following brief tips ought to get you started on the right path. Some of the advice I share is meant to help the person you see in the mirror.

* It's better to have a player who won't do what you say than it is to have one who will only do what you say. The person who has the gall to sometimes disregard your advice is willing to take chances. Football games are won on big plays made by guys who took chances.

* If I gave a direction and my players didn't follow it, I didn't explain myself well enough.

* You're only as strong as your weakest link. You have to coach from where your weakest link is. If a guy's doing the very best he can do, you have to help him. There are always ways you can help players.

* Remain accountable. If I sent in a play and it didn't work, I didn't send in the right play. Coach Bryant always started his

team meetings by admitting his mistakes, and then he'd point out ours. If I take my share of the blame, and you do, too, we can push this wagon out of the mud.

*Always speak plainly and in no uncertain terms.

*Make time to spend time with your teammates, coworkers, friends and family – and make sure you do things they like doing.

*Above all else, associate with Jesus Christ. Lean on Him for your big and small decisions. The more you do, the more you'll find yourself surrounded by people who are winners.

CHAPTER 7

THE NFL WAY

"In his heart a man plans his course, but the Lord determines his steps." – Proverbs 16:9.

I
f you boil my coaching career down to one game, to one moment that illustrates what I did best and what I stood for, look to the Divisional Round of the 1979 AFC Playoffs. This was my moment to stand in the sun. We – the Houston Oilers – were the visiting team in San Diego for a midday game, and I don't remember a brighter sky than the one overhead come game time. On a day like this, not even a cowboy hat can keep the shine out of your eyes. As the stadium roared with the screams of rabid Chargers fans, I couldn't help but reminisce about how I made it to that game.

In football terms, defense was what I became best known for. When I accepted Sid Gillman's offer to coach the Chargers defense in 1967, I installed my 3-4 defense, a scheme which uses three down linemen and four linebackers. Most teams at the time used the 4-3 defense. Well, I'd talked Gillman into running the 3-4 and we did really well with it – at least in the preseason. When the regular season rolled around, Gillman said he wanted to switch. We lost the first game, but he never changed his mind about my defensive scheme. We stayed in the 4-3.

Three years after Gillman resigned from the Chargers in 1971 – and thus virtually resigned for all us assistant coaches – he landed the head coaching job in Houston. He asked me to become the defensive coordinator there, too. Before I said yes, I asked him for his word he'd let me install the 3-4 permanently. He agreed and I moved to Houston. We won four of six preseason games using the defense but then lost to Minnesota 55-6 midway through the regular season. He ordered me to change the defense and blamed the loss on my scheme. The next game, we were losing to the Cardinals 28-0 by halftime, and we switched back to my scheme. We lost 28-21, but the Cardinals didn't score again, and my defense was left alone.

In 1975, Gillman resigned from the Houston job and I became general manager and the Oilers' ninth head coach in its 16-year history. My Oilers in the mid 1970s were the first NFL team to employ the 3-4 full-time. By 1978, 19 teams used the scheme, and many still do today. It's a great way to utilize defensive linemen and linebackers, it's easy to run and you can disguise who rushes and who drops back into coverage. You can also take advantage of the strengths of your personnel. I needed every advantage I could get if we were going to beat San Diego in the 1979 playoffs.

By the time we'd reached those playoffs, I'd lived through the ups and downs of NFL life. Four years before – my first year as a head coach – we went 10-4 and became the surprise story of the league. The national media swarmed on the city, and local news outlets suddenly had interesting story lines to share with their viewers and readers. Who would have thought my cowboy hat, jokes during press conferences and winning streak would have launched me to such fame? NFL Films and other press outlets recorded me riding horses, mingling with the city folk and trying on cowboy boots. I used to take an annual trip to Juarez, Mexico, to see my friend at Sandy Sanders' boot factory – and TV cameras followed. Sandy gave me a free pair or two every time I visited, and I think we both made out on the deal. Most every story or news reel they did on me had something to do with my Western ways. In Houston, a cattle and oil city, I guess it just kind of caught on.

"The timing of the thing … the whole era was kind of Western," Wade, my son, said. "And here was Dad standing on the sideline with a cowboy hat on. It was a great time and everybody was so excited about the team. The fans embraced us so much."

When I took over the Oilers, the team was largely known for being one of the league's worst. In 1972 and 1973, the team had consecutive 1-13 seasons and was outscored 827-363. In 1974, my first year as defensive coordinator, we went 7-7. My first year as head coach, we went 10-4, posted our first winning season in roughly a decade and the city and the team suddenly fell in love with one another.

My first trade as a head coach in 1975 was for Carl Mauck, a fiery center and a friend I'd made when I coached for the Chargers. I then drafted Robert Brazile, who became the NFL's Defensive Rookie of the Year.

In 1978 – after two mediocre years – we wanted to draft a strong offensive player. One day, we were sitting in a meeting and I pointed to a name we had written on a whiteboard.

"What about this guy up here – Earl Campbell?" I said. "I've got one question for you: Do you think he's the best player you've ever seen?"

King Hill, who sat next to my son, Wade, said, "I can't say he isn't."

Everyone looked at each other like Hill was crazy, but I figured we ought to give Campbell a look. I sent Wade to meet Campbell. While my son was one of my youngest coaches, and although his specialty was defense, he always had a knack for spotting talent. I knew Campbell was the type of runner we wanted, but I didn't know if he was the type of guy we wanted. After Wade's visit, my son said Campbell was the kind of guy we wanted and we zeroed in on the University of Texas running back.

Well, we didn't have the No. 1 pick – thus slim hope of landing Campbell – and we needed guys on defense, too. Just before the draft, I sent Wade to Notre Dame.

"I go to Notre Dame and I'm looking at all the defensive players. I do my job. I watch film of every game they played that year, and I looked at nine players who played on defense," Wade said.

During Notre Dame's last game of the season, the Fighting Irish stuffed Campbell – held him to fewer than 100 yards on the ground. Some in football figured maybe Campbell wasn't as good as was once thought. Wade saw something different.

"Texas wasn't blocking well," Wade said. "Campbell made some of the most impressive 3- or 4-yard runs I'd ever seen."

While Wade studied film, his phone rang. His wife, Laurie, called.

"Isn't that great?" she said. "We got Earl Campbell."

"What are you talking about?" Wade said.

"We moved up to the first place in the draft," Laurie replied. "We got Earl Campbell."

"Hey! Hey!" Wade yelled. "We got him!"

We traded for the draft rights to Campbell, and the young running back rewarded us with some of the most electrifying, physical runs in the history of pro football. He once hit a defender so hard his jersey virtually exploded off his body.

Campbell finished his rookie season in 1978 with 1,450 yards, the Rookie of the Year and Offensive Player of the Year honors, and we reached the AFC Championship game. We did so with 21 free agents, who comprised about half the team.

We lost the 1978 AFC Championship game, however, 34-5 to the Pittsburgh Steelers in frigid Three Rivers Stadium.

For a short time we were devastated – until we returned to 50,000 loyal fans who waited for us at the Astrodome. They cheered, lifted our spirits and held "Luv Ya Blue" signs, the city's rallying cry.

An era was born.

After reaching the playoffs for the first time since 1969, the Oilers signed me to a three-year contract. Life was good. That we made it back to the playoffs in 1979 was icing on the cake.

When the NFL has only 28 teams, as it did in 1979, you mathematically have a better chance of winning the lottery than of becoming a pro football coach. To make the NFL playoffs, especially two years in a row, can seem just as daunting. Nothing seemed quite as daunting, though, as the odds the media gave us to beat the San Diego Chargers at their home. Heck, if we listened to the media, we might have just stayed home.

The Chargers were 21-point favorites and the AFC Division Champions. The offensive system San Diego employed was dubbed "Air Coryell" in honor of the team's pass-happy coach, Don Coryell. Dan Fouts, Coryell's quarterback, broke records for passing yards during the regular season. The team passed almost every down, and with receivers who posed a deep threat every play, San Diego could attack with lightning speed. I'm sure the yellow electric bolt on their helmets scared a lot of defenses, but not ours.

If we were going to beat the Chargers on this day, it would be because of our defense. Faced off against the league's most potent passing attack, we lacked the offensive firepower to keep pace. We were without our three offensive stars: Earl Campbell, our brutish running back; Dan Pastorini, our fiery, playboy quarterback; and Kenny Burrough, our confident, deep threat receiver. We lost our stars to injury. As a sign of the challenge we faced, our backup running back arrived at the team hotel on crutches. We were, by any definition, the underdogs, a role I learned to relish and thrive in throughout my career.

Despite the tens of thousands of fans who wore Chargers jerseys in the stands, I didn't feel like an outsider in San Diego. I was there more than 30 years before when I trained as a U.S. Marine in nearby Camp Pendleton. Thanks to those cussing, yelling drill sergeants, San Diego became the place where I learned how *not* to coach people. I'd returned this day to the city where I'd already earned stripes of all sorts, and I was confident I could put those skills to use.

I must admit, this game is my favorite of any I ever coached. The date was Dec. 29, 1979, and I only recently watched it again in its entirety – almost 30 years later to the date. The week before we played San Diego, we defeated the Denver Broncos 13-7 in our first home playoff game since 1962. The win proved costly. Campbell hurt his groin during a first-half touchdown run. Pastorini injured his groin in the second half during a rollout to avoid a blitz. Burrough was slowed by a tailbone bruise and he also re-injured his nagging groin injury. I felt this trio of injuries like a kick to the groin myself.

Still, we defeated the Broncos by holding them to a touchdown. Our defense got after Denver's quarterback, Craig Morton, and registered five sacks in the second half. We poured on the pressure. Nobody thought we had a chance to do the same to San Diego.

All week leading up to the game, the media asked if I'd change things, if I thought we could win and if so, how we could do it. First, we'd have been the underdog even if Campbell, Pastorini and Burrough played. Second, people too often think you can out-coach a team. Maybe that's true, but I believed we had capable players. We'd done the same thing for 25 weeks, and there was no sense in changing things now. Injuries or not, we came to play our style of football. It was my job to keep the players focused, relaxed and tuned out to the media reports.

"Like I've always told everybody," said Carl Mauck, my center, "the deal with coach is that he had a better perspective on life because he went through things in life: The Great Depression, World War II. Football's a game. It wasn't life or death. He'd seen that. Nothing bothered him much."

We needed Mauck to play one heckuva game and open up even bigger running lanes as a blocker than he did for Campbell. I used to tell my players: "Every man get a man, every good man get two." Mauck took the saying to heart.

On defense, we needed everyone to step up – Vernon Perry, a cornerback, especially so. Nobody in the NFL wanted Perry, but we snatched him from the Montreal Alouettes of the Canadian Football League.

"When I got to Houston's camp, I'd never been in a camp like that before," Perry said. "When I went to Houston, I went into a relaxed camp. You never know who you might see: Willy Nelson, the Gatlin Brothers. It was like I was in Hollywood. Bum took care of us, but he was serious about coaching. He would stand up in that tower and I swear he'd think: 'So long as they're playing, just let them be who they are.' I love him to death, would do anything for him. He's always been like a father to me, a mother, a brother and a sister. And that's good because we had a bunch of outlaws on that team."

The Chargers, on the contrary, were not the brutish, scrappy team we were. They were groomed, flashy, and for many had become an aerial nightmare. Dan Fouts, San Diego's bearded quarterback, was the single-season passing leader that year with more than 4,000 yards, and the team's defense was tough, too. Earlier in the season, San Diego beat Pittsburgh 35-7, and the Steelers were the reigning world champions.

To add to our uphill battle, we were exhausted. While San Diego had a bye week, we had to beat Denver to reach this game. We had a short week of preparation – six days instead of seven – traveled across two time zones to reach California and didn't even reach our hotel until late the night before the game.

Still, San Diego had its weaknesses and we knew it. Fouts threw 24 interceptions in 1979, and we led the league in defense by picking off 34 errant passes. We studied Fouts, his tendencies and snap counts. We knew what to expect.

"We studied so much film I knew if Fouts was calling a pass play or a running play long before he ever snapped the ball," Robert Brazile said.

I began studying film when I coached in high school. When I became head coach of the Oilers, technology wasn't as advanced as it is today. We didn't have digital video; the 16-millimeter film we shot existed in those big round rolls we stored in metal cans. To get ahead of the competition when it came to drafting college kids, we needed to know as much as we could about the best prospects.

One day, I told my coaches to clear out a room and to fill it with racks. For years, our scouts had to purchase game film from colleges, quickly review the tape and then send the reel back to the schools. It was a big expense in terms of both time and money. So, we created a film library of every college prospect. We catalogued the games, knew exactly where we could find film on any player and thus streamlined our process for grading talent. Other NFL teams began to call us and ask if they could visit our library to study the films. I loved moving the sport forward, improving it, and so I agreed.

One day I walked into assistant coach John Paul Young's office.

"I want you to go to Philadelphia next week," I told him. "Sony is going to pitch a new video technology."

The problem with viewing game and practice film was you couldn't see the action when you played the tape in reverse.

Coaches spend a lot of time rewinding plays, seeing how they worked or why they failed. Well, Sony devised technology that allowed us to clearly view footage even if we played it in reverse. They even sent us a camera and video player to test out. We reviewed this new technology to see if it was worth a flip. It was clear, bright and full-color. By the end of the season, I took Young with me to pitch the new technology to the NFL. The NFL decided to use the technology we broke in long before it became the norm, and like our library, the league now distributes digital video of all college games to all teams.

Needless to say, we knew about the Chargers' tendencies by the time we ran onto the field to play in the divisional round playoff game. I'm sure San Diego didn't see us coming.

"Many people don't know about my Dad's innovations in football," Wade said. "He never tooted his own horn."

Minutes before kickoff, I roamed the sideline, calm and quiet. I wore a blue coat jacket and white cowboy hat. I dismissed the media hoopla – the questions, the doubts and criticisms. We were 21-point underdogs, but I'm like any football coach – I figured we'd find a way to win. You can take a coach who is 1-9 and he'll think he will win the tenth and eleventh games. If you don't believe it, you can't sell it to the players. We knew we didn't have our starting quarterback, running back and receiver, but we prepared to win nonetheless. If you can't get ready for this kind of game, you ought not to be in football. The game's magnitude made every practice more meaningful. Our players knew they couldn't make any mistakes and still win. I didn't do anything special or different leading up to the game. I approached it like any other week. You always build your team up as the week goes on because you don't want the players to lose their edge. The trick is to get them to play their best game of the week come kickoff.

The old adage is true: You play like you practice. In football, it really doesn't matter what 10 guys do if one person does the wrong thing. The whole play goes wrong. What I wanted my players to realize is you have to pay for the success you want. I don't care how successful you want to become, you have to pay an appropriate price for it. We paid a price during the week leading up to the game against San Diego.

"All Coach Phillips said was just go out there and do your job," Perry, our cornerback, said. "That week, I didn't feel any pressure – but coach worked us hard. Everybody counted us out. The sports writers came around and talked about the guys who were hurt. Hey, we had a job to do, and that's what we were there to do. We had 50 some kids on the field who believed in each other. We loved each other as a player and as a friend. Besides, the critics failed to realize nobody was hurt on defense."

As is human nature, San Diego probably went into the game a bit cocky. In my mind, the circumstances were perfect for an upset.

At kickoff, it was 70 degrees with clear skies. The 50,000 Charger fans were in full throat. As I looked into the stands at Jack Murphy Stadium, I spotted the San Diego Chicken, fans dressed in blue and yellow and hundreds of signs that read, "Charger Power."

San Diego kicked off amid some of the loudest screaming I've heard, and we returned it to the 25 yard line. We'd begun our fight to reach the AFC Championship Game. Giff Nielson, our backup quarterback, jogged onto the field, gathered the team in the huddle and called a running play. In the huddle, we had guys like Mauck at center, Mike Barber at tight end, and Mike Renfro and Rich Caster at wide receiver.

"Everybody just gutted it out," Mauck said. "Everybody decided we'd push on the same wheel."

We ran the ball on the first play of the game, partly to calm our guys and partly because we wanted to control the clock. San Diego knew we had an unproven, second-year quarterback, no deep threats and only a minimal chance to succeed through the air. We called early runs to setup plays I planned to use later in the game. Plus, we thought we could run the ball. To replace Campbell, I employed four running backs – Rob Carpenter, Tim Wilson, Ronnie Coleman and Boobie Clark (yes, that's his name). The guys who blocked all season for Campbell were healthy and in the mood to pick a fight.

Carpenter, who started in place of Campbell, got the bulk of the carries. On second down, he ran up the middle, cut to the outside and was almost stopped one yard short of a first down. A second effort, though, propelled him forward and Barber signaled first down. Carpenter was a second effort kind of guy, despite badly injuring his ankle during practice. At our hotel the night before the game, he could barely walk and only with crutches. I still clearly remember Carpenter bouncing on one leg and down a set of stairs. He wasn't going to miss this game for anything.

We ran the ball four times in a row, moved the chains again but had yet to quiet the crowd. We only wanted to throw the ball when we had to. San Diego stayed in its base 4-3 defense and kept a number of defenders in the box. They didn't feel it necessary to double up on our receivers or replace run-stuffing linebackers with speedy cover men.

On third down and six, Nielsen dropped back to throw his first pass. The Charger rush swarmed him, but Nielsen stood tall, looked down the field and threw a high pass to Barber, our tight end. Barber had stormed off the line of scrimmage, cut inside a defender with a swim move, turned his head the split second he created separation and reacted like a cat to a butterfly. In a flash, he tipped the high pass with one hand, pushed off a defender and fell back and caught the ball while sitting flat on the ground. First down.

Campbell, Pastorini and Burrough paced on the sideline. Pastorini, as always, was energized and yelling encouragement to the team.

Nielsen, on the other hand, quietly and thoughtfully called the next play. The stadium was still electric despite our first down. We ran the ball two more times and faced third down and 3. We lined up with two backs in the backfield. Clark went in motion, but was called for a false start. I wasn't a fan of Ben Dreith, the referee. Of all the league's refs, he was the only one who I thought was against me. His call forced our team into an early third-and-long, and Nielsen into passing again. Excited, he threw the ball high again to Barber, who tipped it as he did during his first catch. This time, though, Barber couldn't corral the pass, and we had to punt. Even though we didn't score, we calmed our nerves, moved the ball and pinned San Diego deep after a fair catch at the 18 yard line.

While we set out to run the ball, San Diego's first offensive play, by contrast, was a pass. Fouts missed his receiver – short-hopped a ball to Charlie Joyner, who was wide open at the 30 – but everyone received the message. The Chargers became division champs by passing the ball, and they had no plans to change this day.

Fouts was a mature, strong-armed quarterback – the type of guy you want running an offense if you need to score. Despite his tendency to also throw interceptions, he scored so often he easily erased mistakes. His receivers, too, were something else. Joyner finished the regular season with 72 catches; John Jefferson had 61 catches and 10 touchdowns. Fouts also had an offensive line that boasted two big, strong Pro Bowlers. They protected Fouts all year like he was the door to a refrigerator full of beer and meat.

My Columbia blue-clad defenders swarmed a Charger receiver, who caught the next pass for an eight-yard gain. On third and 2, Fouts faked a handoff and threw a high arching toss that dropped in and over our defensive back and right into the hands of Gregg McGrary, San Diego's second tight end. McGrary caught the 40-yard-plus pass and suddenly the Chargers were in our territory.

Fouts became frustrated when he overthrew a receiver and then angry when Lydell Mitchell dropped a pass on the next play. On third and long, Fouts threw it again, zipped the pass between two defenders and hit a receiver for a first down at our 26.

With 6:48 remaining in the first quarter, the Chargers ran the ball for the first time, and the fans booed. I still chuckle. San Diego was the first team ever to make the playoffs by passing the ball more than they ran the ball, and the fans offered a roaring reminder.

Taking the verbal cue from the crowd, San Diego moved the ball through the air and to our 14 yard line. During the play, we incurred a face masking penalty, and the refs walked the ball to the 6. A quick Charger score would only pump up the crowd even more, make it increasingly difficult for Nielsen to call plays on offense and immediately put us in a hole. But Fouts surprised everyone by handing the ball to Mitchell, who weaved his way to the 1 yard line. The "Howitzer," Hank Bauer, then scored on a straight-ahead run.

Things looked grim, and I'm not afraid to say so.

BUM LESSON: If you want something, prepare to sacrifice for it.

No greater lesson about sacrifice exists than the one shared by God. He offered to us His only son so you and I have a path to heaven. Jesus died on the cross so our sins can be forgiven.

If you want to reach heaven, you have to sacrifice certain behaviors, thoughts and actions. You also have to accept Christ as your savior.

If you want to succeed elsewhere in life, you must similarly sacrifice. You have to sacrifice leisure time, distractions and laziness. You also better want something badly enough to sacrifice whatever it takes to attain it. Otherwise, you won't have the stamina.

During my early years as a head coach, I sacrificed my off-seasons. I came up with the idea to entice college football's best prospects to meet in one place – and thus negate the need for me and my coaches to travel all across the country. We filmed college athletes while we worked them out at each position, and soon five clubs joined us. The league's front office became so fond of the idea they took it over after a few years. The NFL Network and other sports networks now broadcast the NFL Combine on TV.

No matter what you do, practice all week – in matters big and small – to win. This is what differentiates people who want to win and those who just want to win a little bit. I don't know but one philosophy: Do what you're supposed to do when you're supposed to do it. Then, no matter how badly the odds are stacked against you, you never give up.

If you do that, you'll succeed. Win or lose, you'll look back and realize the scoreboard doesn't always tell the whole story.

CHAPTER 8

THE WAY TO TRUST

"When I am afraid, I will trust in you." Psalm 56:3

I n both football and life, trust is more important than you know. Despite falling behind by a first quarter touchdown to the Chargers, we never lost sight of that. San Diego kicked off, and we returned the ball to the 22. On the first play of our second series, Nielsen dropped back, shuffled his feet to 12 yards behind the line of scrimmage to avoid the rush and threw an ugly, incomplete pass. Carpenter then ran the ball for a short gain, and the next play he caught a screen pass short of a first down. We had to punt again, and the San Diego Chicken ran through the crowd with a "Charger Power" sign, exciting the fans and rewarding a stout defense.

The Chargers came back with their West Coast-styled offense, in essence what it was before the scheme was ever called that. Many of Fouts' short passes – dump-offs to running backs – became extensions of handoffs. They mixed screen passes, long passes and intermediate throws and, before we knew it, had the ball just beyond the 50 yard line.

Fouts was 5 for 8 for 76 yards, commanding and fierce. He dropped back to pass again but this time heaved one he shouldn't have. He overthrew Jefferson deep down the right sideline, and Vernon Perry intercepted it.

As I mentioned, we'd found Perry earlier in the year by scanning film of Canadian professional football players. Perry's interception was an amazing omen of things to come – evidence that the trust we had in each other would lift us – and a sign this wounded team of underdogs was primed to do something nobody but us thought we could do.

"When I grabbed my first interception off Fouts, I said, 'Oh, yeah. That gets us off the field. Thank you, Jesus,'" Perry said. "For some reason, I was going to have a great day."

We now moved left to right if you watched the game on TV, but the view from the sideline did not change a whole lot once the second quarter started.

Perry's first quarter, momentum-changing interception failed to kick start our offense. We gained one first down after the interception, but then ran into a wall on third and short. Our offense didn't appear it could move the ball with any consistency. We punted and downed the ball at San Diego's 31 yard line.

Nielsen, our backup quarterback, jogged to the sideline. I could tell he shook the first-quarter jitters and settled into his role for the game. Quarterbacks must trust their coaches to call the right play, their offensive linemen to ward off blitzers and their receivers to run precise routes. Nielsen always called the play I sent in to be run, and he trusted me to call the right play. Other players similarly rely on this blind trust. If one man misses an assignment, the play can fail.

Trust in football goes even deeper.

Nielsen had every reason to remain nervous. He had read the newspaper reports, listened to the sports analysts poke holes in his experience and, no doubt, felt the pressure. I'd drafted Nielsen the year before, in 1978, and called him to say so. He was tall, talented and articulate – just the type of guy you wanted to back up Dan Pastorini. Nielsen, a Brigham Young University graduate, realized a boyhood dream.

"I picked up Coach's phone call, and in his Texas drawl, he said, 'Is Giff Nielsen there? This is Bum Phillips with the Houston Oilers. We just drafted you on our team,'" Nielsen said. "I flew down to Houston and he certainly did not look like a football coach. He was one of the most interesting-looking guys I'd ever seen in my life. He had on these pointed cowboy boots, but I learned very early on from him the greatest lesson I could have learned from anyone: to trust. He kept preaching it to me. He'd say, 'Just trust me and great things will happen.'"

Nielsen's first start in the NFL was during the preseason against the Dallas Cowboys, his favorite team as a boy. I told him he'd start; we wanted to see if he could play in the NFL and if everything was going to be OK.

"Just trust me," I said.

We learned three hugely valuable lessons that night: We could beat Dallas, Earl Campbell, who we also drafted that year, was going to be an NFL great one day and Giff Nielsen was exactly the backup quarterback we needed.

"After the game, coach came up to me and he put his arms around me," Nielsen said. "He said, 'That was outstanding. What you did today was just great. You proved we can now count on you as our backup quarterback.' He made me feel like I was No. 1 in his life. I knew I wasn't, but he made me feel like I was. The level of trust he put in me is a lesson I learned and still use in my life. He trusted that we'd get ourselves ready to play against San Diego in the playoffs. He trusted us during the course of the game. I was just telling a group yesterday about the importance of trust and how much I appreciate Bum for teaching me that."

Earlier in the 1979 season, Pastorini got hurt and Nielsen stepped in against Kansas City. We beat the Chiefs 20-6.

Every now and then someone steps up like Nielsen did, and we counted on him to do so again in San Diego. Playing in only his second game outside the preseason, he had the added pressure of starting in the playoffs.

After football, Nielsen became a 25-year, award-winning TV sports broadcaster in Houston, and today he is the president of the Houston Texas South Stake of The Church of Jesus Christ of Latter-day Saints. He's a real champion in every way. The kid didn't cuss, smoke or drink, and he was a huge star at Brigham Young University. He had such a great temperament and he could take everything the critics said and just deal with it.

"Coach knew how to motivate me, too," Nielsen said. "I mentioned we won the preseason game against Dallas. Well, to fire me up, he later gave a speech to the team. 'Heck,' he said. 'We beat Dallas without a quarterback. Why can't we win this one?'"

San Diego had the ball at its own 31 yard line with 12:11 remaining in the second quarter, and as predicted went right back to the passing game. Fouts' first pass moved the chains, and so did his second and third. In a flash, the Chargers moved the ball 38 yards and well into our territory. Down 7-0 and with San Diego on the move, we were in danger of falling quickly into an even deeper hole.

Our defense then began to apply pressure on Fouts. He threw a quick pass, which a receiver dropped. Then we blitzed, guessing they'd run a draw play – and it worked. If we could hold San Diego to a field goal attempt, we'd chalk this series up as a success. We'd only be down by 10 points, and a lucky break on offense could move us to within one score by halftime.

On third down and 12, Fouts, though, bought time in the pocket and drilled a pass for a first down. He moved the ball to just inside the 20. The San Diego Chicken ran through the stands again, inciting the already-raucous crowd.

Feeling the pressure our defense applied to his quarterback, Don Coryell then went to the run – first, a run play for seven yards and then one for three. We were backed up at the 10 yard line, and San Diego had a first down and goal. Lydell Mitchell ran for four yards on the tenth play of the drive, which began almost 60 yards down the field. Our guys were gassed, sucking wind, but as of yet bending and not breaking.

Finally, Andy Dorris broke into the backfield and leveled the runner for a two-yard loss. Dorris hit Mitchell, lifted him off the ground and dropped him on his rear. Dorris had bounced around from team to team, but found a home and flourished with the group we formed in Houston.

Fouts dropped back to pass on third down and fired a bullet toward the center of the field, but the pass was deflected. San Diego's field goal unit marched onto the field. Mike Wood, San Diego's kicker, hadn't missed a field goal from inside the 50 yard line since becoming a Charger. Certainly, he wouldn't miss from about the 10 yard line.

Perry, our rookie who'd picked off Fouts in the first quarter, lined up on the edge. His thighs burned from the long drive he'd just helped to defend against, and he wondered if he'd have the energy to burst forward at the snap. He put his hand on the ground, darted a step to his outside and then sprung inside just as Wood approached the kick. Perry leaped high into the air, blocked the kick with outstretched arms and fell back to his feet in one smooth motion. As if he had a magnet pinned to his chest, the ball bounced up perfectly and into his arms. With no one in front of him, Perry ran as fast as he could. He passed the 20, the 30, 40 and 50. He sprinted beyond half field with a clear path to score.

Players still tease him about what happened next.

"You have to understand," Perry said, "San Diego drove the ball all the way down to the 10 yard line. I was exhausted. Coach Phillips always told me to jump over that receiver and go in and block the kicks. I blocked it and I was off to the races."

A Charger player caught Perry at the San Diego 29 yard line, tackled the tired cornerback and stopped a would-be touchdown.

"My teammates still say, 'You got run down by a white boy,'" Perry said, laughing. "They'd just marched all the way down the field, and now you want me to run 90 yards the other way? I was too darned tired."

Perry's play invigorated our team. For the first time, San Diego's home-field advantage sounded more like an abandoned warehouse than a packed stadium. The crowd was quiet and you could hear cheers from our sideline over the roars the chicken spurred earlier.

Our offense took the field, and we immediately went to Rob Carpenter. It hurt to watch him run on his injured ankle, and I couldn't get the image of him on crutches the night before out of my mind. Carpenter played courageously and selflessly this day. Had it not been for Earl Campbell, he'd have been our starter. With each of his strides you could see the limp in his sprint, but in two plays he moved the ball to the 15. He ran hurt, but he ran hard. He was our miracle man, and he repeatedly carried tacklers for extra yards.

I remember looking down our sideline, a feeling of pride in my belly, and watching Pastorini pace near the field. He stared out at the offense he'd become accustomed to commanding, and never once did he let his injury turn him sour to Nielsen or the team. He relieved stress by running his throwing hand through his hair and yelling encouragement to his friends on the field.

On third down, Nielsen missed an open receiver and Toni Fritsch, our pudgy Pro Bowl kicker, waddled onto the field.

Fritsch had played nine games for the Austrian Men's National Soccer Team, and he'd moved to the United States during a time when soccer-styled kickers were popular. I later brought Fritsch to New Orleans with me when I became head coach of the Saints in the early 1980s. He was one kicker I could trust.

Fritsch drilled home the short field goal and we narrowed San Diego's lead to 7-3. With 4:02 remaining in the first half, I looked up, lost in my thoughts about the next defensive series, and squinted to make sure my eyes hadn't deceived me. In a sea of Chargers fans, I saw a man who held a Luv Ya Blue sign. The image of this one man, rooting for our underdog team in the middle of a Charger storm, somehow resonated with me. We were in this stadium, going toe-to-toe with the favorites. Just like our fan, we began to show our true colors. We started to fight back.

I often taught my teams lessons about the importance of fighting, of never giving up. Too often, people throw in the towel when things get tough. You must remember the scoreboard doesn't always reflect who won and lost, and that's true in sports and in life.

"Coach always taught us you have to battle back – no matter what," Carl Mauck, our starting center, said. "Sometimes, the little things eat people up. Well, Bum used to tell us this story: This guy got shot on one of the islands when he served during World War II, and the guy was pretty bad off. He had to lay wounded out in the hot sun for hours. Finally, he got picked up. They loaded him on a seaplane, which the Japanese then shot down into the water. Finally, a boat came by and they pulled him from the wreckage. On that same day, another guy got nicked and he died in three or four hours. He wasn't even badly hurt. Well, when Bum got back to the States, he often wondered about the guy who was shot and then shot down. He ran into him at Stephen F. Austin University. He said that's the kind of guys you're looking for in life and football."

After our field goal, San Diego took the field with newfound aggression. I think it ticked them off they were only winning 7-3. Fouts looked mad. He dumped a short pass to a running back, but Art Stringer, a 220-pound linebacker who we called the Disco King, made the tackle. Stringer, fittingly enough, hit hard, danced and wrote poetry.

Fouts' next pass was incomplete, and he suddenly faced a third down and nine. He dropped back, threw it 25 yards down the middle of the field and Perry intercepted him – again. Perry read the pass perfectly, and our pressure forced Fouts to release the ball early. On the play, Perry blended instinct and film study into positional awareness. He seemed to know where the ball was headed before it was headed there.

We had the ball at the 39 yard line with three minutes left on the clock. We knew to win we'd need an outstanding performance from the defense, and outside San Diego's first series, our guys delivered.

Like his San Diego counterpart, Nielsen ran onto the field with a different air, too. He ran taller, more confidently, and I saw it clear as day. I called a screen pass, which he completed for five yards.

"C'mon Gifford," Pastorini yelled from the sideline, pacing and cheering.

Nielsen completed another pass to Carpenter, who hurt himself even worse on the play. He bobbled the catch, stood upright to gather it and absorbed no fewer than five hits from as many players. When he snatched the ball, he then spun in an effort to avoid a pile that clamped down on him like wolves on a fresh kill. He hurt his ankle in the melee and writhed on the ground. Flat on his stomach, he slid forward. He finally pulled himself up from a flat, five-yard slide and he hobbled to the sideline. I looked at Nielsen and called another pass play. Clark caught the throw and moved the ball inside the 20.

I'll never forget the next play. Nor will Nielsen or his teammates.

Because we trusted Nielsen, we called another pass play. He was making smart decisions and delivering accurate passes. San Diego, though, blitzed from Nielsen's right side and immediately broke our play design. Nielsen stood tall for a second, bounced, and then felt the pressure. He bolted to his left and from the pocket. He ran around the end, beyond the 15 yard line, then the 10 and moved into a safe lane with nothing between him and the sideline. Instead of running out of bounds, though, he cut inside a defender – pulled off a quarterback version of a juke – and dashed for the endzone. A defender met Nielsen on his cut and leveled him. I don't think I saw a nastier hit than the one Nielsen suffered at the 5 yard line. For a moment, he remained motionless on the ground, woozy and wondering if he'd get up. Fans back in Houston suddenly wondered who our third string quarterback was. Pastorini, who could barely jog, ran onto the field, fiery-eyed and ready to step in. I didn't have problems with my heart until 2005, but Giff Nielsen almost forced them prematurely upon me when he took that hit.

"I felt a little bit of pressure from the backside, wheeled out to the left side and I'm thinking, 'I'm going to score,'" Nielsen said. "I wasn't the fastest guy in the world, and when I ran out there I was pretty much by myself. I might be 10 yards beyond the line of scrimmage, so I'm thinking I'll go out to the sideline and see what I can get. Then I have this scary thought: *I'm the only quarterback.* For some reason, I did the stupidest thing I ever did in my life. I decided I was going to try to score. I cut back inside. San Diego had a little safety and he hit me in the lower back so hard I thought I'd just ruptured a kidney. My center Carl Mauck, who is not quiet, got on a knee. You have to understand his vocabulary, so I'll be nice. He said, 'Are you OK?' As soon as I said I was OK, he started ripping me up one side and down the other. That didn't help because I couldn't raise my right arm. I went back to the huddle. I couldn't stop because we didn't have anyone else. I waved Pastorini off. We were on the 3 yard line and I wanted us to score a touchdown and to take the lead."

Mauck remembers Nielsen's run, too.

"Next time get your big 'bleep' out of bounds," Mauck remembers telling his backup quarterback. "Don't you ever do that again!"

Mauck is the type of guy you want first on your team. After playing for me, he went on to coach for seven NFL teams – including time spent with me as an assistant. During his playing days, he was my on-field general and off-the-field enforcer.

Nielsen was still in pain, but he refused to leave the game. He stood in the huddle, hands on his hips, and awaited our next play call. With about one minute on the clock and in position to score, the pain of the hit he suffered at the 5 yard line was not enough to sideline him. Carpenter, though, could barely move after he re-injured his ankle, and I opted to send in Clark. Twice we ran it to Clark, and San Diego stopped him both times. The Chargers had to know Nielsen was in no shape to throw, so they played against the run, stacked the box and dared us to hand it off again.

On third down and goal from the 1 yard line, we called a play-action pass. We'd successfully run down the clock to 29 seconds, and no matter what happened, San Diego would have little time to drive down the field.

Nielsen took the snap, turned around as if he would hand the ball to Clark and then quickly pulled the ball back and spun to face the rush. He threw it to Mike Barber, our tight end who was wide open in the back of the endzone. Barber, though, lost his balance, stumbled and missed the catch as he fell to the ground. On fourth down and 1, we sent Fritsch on to kick a field goal. If he made it, we'd narrow San Diego's lead to 7-6.

Fritsch jogged onto the field, lined up behind the holder and kicked the ball straight through the uprights. I threw my hands up in the air in excitement and then saw a yellow flag on the ground. Referees called San Diego for being offside, which would move the ball half the distance to the goal line. We could decline the penalty and accept the three points or accept the penalty and go for it from the half-yard line.

Up until this point in the game, we played conservatively. We ran the ball consistently, avoided forcing too much onto Nielsen and relied heavily on our defense.

Statistically, San Diego had 12 first downs to our eight, and 149 passing yards to Nielsen's 46 on seven completions. We had won three key categories thus far, though: turnovers, time of possession and rushing yards. We had the ball for 16 minutes and committed no turnovers; San Diego had the ball for 14 minutes and lost three turnovers – including the blocked field goal. On the ground, we compiled 71 rushing yards, about twice as many as San Diego earned.

If we were going to grab and maintain a lead, we had to chip away at the Chargers' score and keep Fouts off the field. I called a timeout to give my decision more thought. Nielsen ran to the sideline and we talked about it.

"What do you want to do?" I said.

Pastorini limped toward Nielsen in obvious pain. When Pastorini ruptured his right groin muscle the week before, he said he heard a pop that sounded like a gunshot, and his leg was still purple from his hip to his ankle.

"I just kept trying to keep Gifford playing within himself. He was playing a beautiful game," Pastorini said. "I told him, 'You're out there in a huddle with cutthroats, rapists and thieves. Don't be afraid to swear if you have to. Also, don't you ever run the ball like that again. You throw it away next time.'"

After a few moments, we decided to go for it.

"We've got to score a touchdown," I told Nielsen.

I'm not sure if San Diego expected us to erase three points from the scoreboard on account of being a half-yard closer to the goal line, but you could feel the tension in the stadium. The fans cheered louder than ever as Nielsen led the group to the line of scrimmage.

Without Earl Campbell and with Carpenter and Nielsen still too banged up to run – even a quarterback sneak – we turned again to Boobie Clark. He was a big back, gray-haired and far from being the fastest guy on the team. We were sure San Diego expected us to run him straight up the gut, so we called a 39 toss, a pitch to Clark. He'd get the ball on a sweeping arc and take it to the left side of our line and outside the tackle box. We hoped to catch San Diego on its inside stunts.

Nielsen snapped the ball, turned to his left and tossed the ball to Clark, who veered in a semi-arch to the outside left. A San Diego cornerback, though, cut the lane to the outside and forced Clark to move quickly inside. He made a sharp cut, found a crease and plowed ahead toward the goal line.

Clark bulldozed his way into the endzone, thanks in large part to Mauck. Mauck pulled from his center position and dropped a linebacker on the outside, which opened a hole big enough for Clark to squeeze through.

Nobody would have believed the halftime score line before the game, but we were up 10-7.

"That's Bum," Nielsen said. "When people lacked confidence in us, he didn't. That touchdown set up the dramatics of the second half. I could go on and on and on, but let me just say he's had an amazing influence on my life. Consequently, he influenced my children, my family, everyone I'm around. I am a product of Bum Phillips."

By halftime, we had the lead and the momentum. Perry had two interceptions, a blocked field goal and a long return. We took a gamble on fourth down and goal from a short distance, and it paid off. If we needed luck to beat San Diego, we made our own.

"Here we were playing the highest-scoring team in the league. It was supposedly their year to knock off the Steelers," Nielsen said. "We go out there with all these injuries. I had very limited experience playing quarterback and here comes Bum again: 'Just trust me.' All week, Bum said, 'Trust me, we're going to win this game with defense. And, Giff, when you have a shot, you have to take it.' We went out there and it was David and Goliath. Once again, Bum's fingerprints were all over it."

Even from the sideline, and despite the frustration he felt because he couldn't play, Pastorini saw what millions of TV watchers began to witness, too.

"We knew we weren't good alone, but together we were great," Pastorini said. "Never underestimate the heart of a champion."

My heart would be tested again in the second half, though. San Diego had no plans to give up. Neither did Perry. Our rookie cornerback, whom we'd plucked out of Canadian obscurity, was about to do something nobody could have seen coming.

BUM LESSON: Build people up; don't tear them down.

No matter what you do in life – whether your job is in sports, corporate America or at home with your family – I can't stress enough the importance of encouraging those around you.

If you believe in someone, especially when they don't believe in themselves, you help to give them an amazing gift: confidence.

Andrea, my daughter who teaches and coaches a swim team, gravitated toward her career because, like me, she loves to encourage people.

"That was Dad's gift as a coach – to make every player, first string to benchwarmer, feel they are important to the team," Andrea said. "This is one way Dad got everyone to give their best and be ready to play their heart out any time he needed them."

My son, Wade, is cut from the same cloth. He coaches the Dallas Cowboys and is often criticized by the media for treating players well.

"The image of a football coach has always been that you scream and holler, and get in their face to make them better," Wade said. "But Daddy always thought and taught that teaching was the most important thing. Lead a horse to water instead of trying to push him there. Cussing out a guy doesn't make them better. Because of my Dad and because I think he coached the right way, I believe I coach the right way."

If those around you offer criticism rather than praise, my son encourages you to remain strong. While he earned the trust of the Cowboys ownership and players, he can speak firsthand about dealing with constant condemnation. You can argue that the press scrutinizes the Dallas Cowboys more than it does any other sports team in the world.

"You don't judge yourself by what others say or think," Wade said. "You have to work hard at what you do, believe in what you're doing and enjoy what you're doing. Now, if my Dad said I wasn't doing a good job, that's one thing. But I don't listen to what the press says about me."

CHAPTER 9

A FOOTBALL FAMILY'S WAY

"How good and pleasant it is when brothers live together in unity!" – Psalm 133:1.

My halftime speech to the players was simple: "I have faith in each and everyone one of you."

We'd amassed a lead and were confident we could fight off a San Diego comeback. It helped to look out in the locker room at the sea of Columbia-blue Oilers jerseys and at the faces of the men who wore them. Each man possessed the type of character we sought during my days in Houston. We had a near-perfect mix of young and old, talented and role players – like most teams, really. What separated us in my mind was how close we were as a team. We took the field in the second half as friends and family.

"I think everyone was excited," Wade, my son and assistant defensive coach, said. "We had to calm them down a little bit. It was loud when we got into the locker room. My Dad said, 'Let's go back and do the same thing.' He could have really mishandled it there, too. If a team gets too excited and the coach goes crazy, it can hurt the performance. His calming effect really helped."

The sun hit my face as we emerged from the tunnel, but the rim of the stadium began to cast a shadow over the field as the afternoon wore on. The crowd reawakened when Fouts jogged onto the field, and we knew going into the third quarter we'd have to play even better to maintain our 10-7 lead.

Ted Washington, our outside linebacker, had seven career interceptions but let one slip on the first play of the second half. Fouts threw an intermediate pass and the ball hit Washington in the hands, but he dropped it. Like the shadow creeping across midfield, the dropped interception served as an omen of early third-quarter things to come.

Momentum is key in football, and halftime breaks can work for or against you. San Diego benefited, it seemed, because the team moved the ball right down the field. I think it helped the Chargers had a bye week before our game, and thus extra time to pick holes in our defense.

Fouts found his stride. He dropped back, bounced and found time and space to step forward and drive passes into receivers. Don Coryell, who wore a scowl and blue checker-print pants, paced the opposite sideline. Within a blink, they had the ball at our 10 yard line, and Lydell Mitchell ran a surprise handoff in for a touchdown. The Charger cannon fired, an emphatic end to a 65-yard, 1:42 drive.

You never know before the game how the dynamics will play out. We knew we might find ourselves trailing the Chargers, so before kickoff I delivered a message to the team that resonated, especially when San Diego recaptured the lead.

"During a team meeting before the game, he brought in a newspaper," Wade said. "He held it up and said, 'Here's the San Diego paper.' The headlines said we'd lose. My Dad said, 'When you underestimate your opponent, you're going to get your rear beat. This article doesn't say one thing about us or this game. It's all about the Chargers. They're going to get their rears beat tomorrow.'"

Needing to reignite our momentum, we lined up our star receiver, Kenny Burrough, on the outside. Burrough didn't play the first half because of injury. We put him in during the second half as a decoy. His first appearance came on a run play – and it worked. Tim Wilson, who typically played fullback and blocked for Earl Campbell, played backup running back and moved the ball to the 50 yard line on two rushes. With Burrough in the formation, San Diego lined up in a deep coverage set expecting to defend a pass, and we made the team pay by running right at it.

We committed a penalty, however – our fourth for a total of 40 yards – and our once-promising drive stalled. As we lined up to punt, the fans stood, screamed and applauded. I clapped on our sideline and encouraged my team. Cliff Parsley offered his own style of encouragement.

Up until this kick, Parsley averaged about 41 yards a punt – a solid average. On this kick, he dropped the ball at the 10 yard line in the middle of the field and it bounced in one hop to the 1. Then, the ball magically caromed in a straight line all the way along the goal line and out of bounds at the 2. He pinned San Diego deep and forced Fouts to face a long field. While we trailed again 14-10, we received the kick start we needed.

Anchored by a strong defensive outing, we forced a San Diego punt for the first time this game. Punter Jeff West stood in the endzone while rookie Richard Ellender waited at midfield. Ellender had returned punts 31 times this season and averaged just more than six yards per return, but he outdid himself on this one. Ellender caught the ball at the 50, weaved his way through a mad rush of defenders and made his way to the 23. We huddled on offense already in field goal position.

A man in the stands held a sign: "Strike Oil," it read, a reference to beating us.

After two runs, it was third down and seven from the 20. Burrough lined up again on one side of the field as a decoy for a pass we planned to throw to the other.

Nielsen dropped back, feinted to his right and tossed a ball deep into the left corner of the endzone. Richard Caster was open, but Nielsen overthrew him and San Diego intercepted the ball. Nielsen didn't notice Caster was double-covered, and the throw cost us at least three points.

When I remember back to moments such as these, I look to a piece of artwork hanging on a wall in my Goliad home. Above my TV and near the fireplace – where my wife and I also positioned 36 spurs – is a painting of cowboys who sing and play guitar while gathered around a campfire somewhere on the nighttime range. The painting's nice to look at it, but I think it symbolizes the type of team we were, too: A bunch of guys who liked hard work, fun and being around each other.

The Chargers had scored on their opening drives of both halves, and Nielsen had thrown an interception, but we didn't fall apart as a team. In fact, we rallied around each other like cowboys might after a long day moving cattle down a dangerous trail.

Andy Dorris, our big, run-stopping defensive lineman, agrees. He was our type of guy. He worked hard and enjoyed doing it – even had a pet lion. We accepted each others' personality quirks and rose as teammates even after one of us erred.

"We were playing in New England one year and we were behind up there 24-3 at halftime," Dorris said. "I had three 15-yard penalties: two roughing the passer penalties and a hit out of bounds. Bum came in and talked to us at halftime. He said, 'Well, this game ain't going the way we wanted. During this second half, just go out there and play. We'll pick up the pieces when we get back home. Just go enjoy yourselves.' We all thought he'd given up on us. *We can't let him down.* He knew what he was doing. We went out and won that game. The San Diego game was our kind of game."

I always was more interested in the kind of guy I coached rather than the type of player he was. He didn't have to be a good player, but he had to want to improve himself. He had to believe it was his job to get better. I took pride in taking kids others said couldn't play and molding them into men who could. I enjoyed bragging on them, too, giving them confidence and helping them to play the best they could.

One of my favorite NFL players was Carl Mauck because, like me, he was a country boy. Back in our days in San Diego in the 1960s – on flights home from away games – we sat on the jump seat at the back of the plane, drank beer and played Name That Tune.

"Bum believed that football built a man's character," Mauck said. "He encouraged us to be part of the community. We did a lot of charity work with the Oilers and most of it benefited children. He had us doing that long before it was popular in the league to do so."

While I believed it was our job to give back, I also believed it was my job to create an environment where men of all shapes and sizes gelled into one big, happy family. In the NFL, I implemented a lesson learned when I coached in high school.

I organized my high school practices in great detail – down to the second. This way, we could impart as many lessons as possible in a given time, and the players benefitted from repetitions. Some players didn't respond well to the grinding nature of my schedule, though. Some players lost their joy of the sport.

After practice one day, I mingled with my high school coaching staff in the field house. We dissected practice, visited and planned for the next day. Then, Don Chambers, a standout tackle, knocked on the door. Chambers walked into the room, handed me his jersey and said he quit.

I looked at him, puzzled, and then at the jersey he'd just handed me. I put the jersey back in his hands, my arm on the teen's shoulder and escorted him to the door. I told him he couldn't quit, and then closed the door.

My coaching staff had a good laugh, but I wanted to know why an all-state selection suddenly wanted nothing to do with football. Later, I tracked Chambers down.

"Coach, it's just not fun anymore," Chambers said (1).

"What do you mean it's not fun?" I said. "It's fun when we win, but you've got to pay the price in the off-season to be able to win in the fall. That's when you get your fun."

Chambers insisted my training program – formed from my time with the U.S. Marines – was intolerable. His observation offered new insight. We'd organized the fun right out of football. Our drills were timed so precisely and our whistles blared so often, players lacked the time and energy to joke or talk with other teammates.

The next day, we relaxed our regimen, discarded a few of the more gruesome drills and gave players breaks. We put the fun back into the sport. If you let players enjoy football, they will.

I carried this lesson with me to Houston. I made darned sure my professional players worked hard but still had fun in the process.

"Bum believed if you wanted something in life, you have to pay for it or work for it," Mauck said. "He used to say, 'Good times and hard work go together, but hard work comes first.' I think that is why we were so successful in Houston. We worked hard, but it wasn't drudgery. He made it fun, and he wasn't so uptight, especially about things that really didn't matter."

I received my share of criticism for creating a family atmosphere. Reporters and outsiders believed an NFL head coach ought to wear a fedora and intimidate his players. "Coaches should yell, scream and cuss," they said. This approach wasn't for me and if you ask 99 percent of players, it's not for them either.

In Houston, we threw barbecues, invited music stars to practice and made Saturdays a time for families – wives, children, girlfriends and pets included. Married players tossed a ball to their son or single guys tossed tennis balls to their dogs. Significant others became friends, and the players became closer as well.

If you expect a guy to give something extra, you have to give something extra, too. Thus our Saturday practices resembled company picnics. I never figured you were going to get a whole lot done on a Saturday anyway. You might as well make it a friendly atmosphere.

"People who care about other people will fight harder for them and with them," Wade said. "It goes back to being in the foxhole. They have to be family, someone you believe in. Part of my Dad's success was being accessible, I think. He talked with the players, joked and treated them like men rather than little kids. People are so afraid they'll lose respect for talking with a player, joking with a player. So long as you can coach and teach a player, you earn respect. My Dad believes in it, and I believe in it, too."

Friendship is nothing you can take from a guy. He has to give it. I created situations where guys could get to know each other and become real friends.

You see, to get guys to buy into your system – to get them to play for you and for each other – a coach first has to be himself, and then he ought to become a friend. Every Friday night I brought in live entertainment, and we played dominoes or card games. Musicians often joined us.

"We might be having a barbecue and you'd see Willy Nelson talking to Bum," Vernon Perry said. "You had so much fun you couldn't help but also do your job. You felt respected, appreciated. It was a dream come true. Bum wasn't a spiritual man when he coached us, but the Lord was in his heart. He taught us to love thy neighbor. Now when we see each other, we still give a hug. That's what made us a better team."

We had everything from clean cut and highly educated players to wild cards and men from the inner city, but they became brothers. They'd do anything for each other.

"Bum broke down all the barriers," Pastorini said. "To do so in the Deep South was even more impressive. To this day, we remain a brotherhood."

Robert Brazile became the NFL's Defensive Rookie of the Year in 1975, the year we drafted him.

"Bum made all of us feel like we were his son. It didn't matter what size you were, what color you were, how fast you were," Brazile said. "A person could never say they were homesick with Bum around. I would stay up at nights just to watch him play dominoes. He's the coolest man who ever coached me."

Ronnie Coleman was one of our backup running backs. He received few carries, but we knew we could count on him. During one game, we were losing 13-19 and we put Coleman in to run a sweep. He took the ball on third down and seven, scored a long touchdown and we won the game.

"I ran to the sidelines and coach planted a big kiss on me – and I was sweaty," Coleman said. "Now, I'd never had a man plant a kiss on me before. My Dad didn't kiss me. Bum showed me so much love at that time – it was a moment I'll never forget."

Coleman is now an ordained minister, and I recently spoke for him during a prayer breakfast. Andy Dorris stopped by during a recent hunting trip and watched college football for a few hours. Earl Campbell calls every month or so.

Burrough, Nielsen, Barber, Mauck, Pastorini, Ted Thompson and others visit often, too.

"I still call coach and get advice," Perry said. "He still tells me he loves me. What he did to win and to create a football family ought to get him into the Hall of Fame."

After Nielsen threw the interception, our defense knew it had to step up. The Chargers moved the ball to midfield, but a string of holding penalties forced Fouts to become impatient. On third down and 17, JC Wilson picked him off with one hand. Wilson jumped high into the air and with his right hand grabbed the ball. He danced around during his return and gave us the ball inside the 50.

Nielsen then hit Mike Renfroe on a short pass over the middle of the field. Renfroe, a Pro Bowl receiver, caught the ball running left, but then he turned the other way, bounced right and to the outside and followed blocks all the way down the field. He dove into the endzone, celebrated and pointed thankfully to the down-field blockers, including Ronnie Coleman.

We'd rallied again and led 17-14. Before the game, Don Coryell held a press conference and pleaded with fans to scream and cheer louder than they'd ever done. Even though we'd just stomped San Diego's momentum, the fans came alive again.

After the third quarter ended, we expected nothing but San Diego's best. The Chargers amassed 290 yards in total offense – almost twice as much as we had – but our defense played lights out.

With victory in sight, our offense took the field. Despite his painful ankle injury, Rob Carpenter blasted through the right side, ran over defenders like Earl Campbell would have and willed his way to a first down. I looked at the clock: 12 minutes remaining in the game.

Boobie Clark practiced only one day that week at fullback. He had to switch his position during the playoffs because of injuries. He'd only carried the ball 25 times all year, but he found a way to provide a spark. Hoping to take time off the clock, we ran it twice to Clark and he, too, made a first down. We began moving the ball with every handoff: big chunks and small chunks. Consequently, chunks of time disappeared from the clock.

On third down and eight, we spread the Chargers defense and lined up as if we were going to pass. We ran a surprise draw play to Carpenter, who hobbled for 10 yards.

Finally, San Diego forced us to punt, and Cliff Parsley pinned San Diego deep again. The Charger return man caught Parsley's high, booming punt at the 9.

Coryell wasn't used to losing. He was 20-8 as the Chargers' head coach, and he paced angrily on the sideline. With 6:34 remaining in the game, his offense would have to move the length of the field to regain the lead. As expected, the team went to the air.

After a 16-yard pass play and another for 30, Dorris sacked Fouts for a seven-yard loss. Fouts rebounded with a 17-yard pass and another first down. San Diego had the ball at the 35 and moved close to field goal range.

The very next play, Robert Brazile tipped a pass and Vernon Perry intercepted it. It was Perry's third interception of the day, and Coryell buckled on the sideline. We had a chance to hold the ball and to keep the clock running if we could just make a first down.

Three minutes remained on the clock, which now seemed to tick so slowly.

San Diego had all three of its timeouts. We ran it twice to Carpenter but only gained three yards. The clock ticked to the two-minute warning. If we could make the first down, we'd force San Diego to begin using its timeouts. If not, we'd have to punt and give the ball back to Fouts with a full arsenal of timeouts.

"As everything was unfolding, there was this feeling that this game is ours," Coleman said. "You could see the frustration on the Chargers. I hadn't played a whole lot that year, but coach put me in on third down."

Just as Coleman did earlier in the year, he came in on third down with the game on the line. Nielsen, all 6-foot-4-inches of him, dropped back, pump faked to his right and then threw a bullet across the field and hit Coleman for his first catch of the game. Coleman ran for a first down. Our team cheered and let out a collective sigh of relief. In doing so, we deflated the air in the warm stadium.

San Diego took its first timeout with 1:50 left on the clock. After two consecutive runs, San Diego used its last timeout with 1:32 remaining.

After failing to gain a first down, we had to punt. San Diego would get one last chance to come back, but again Parsley pinned the Chargers deep.

Fouts took the field and gathered his team in the endzone. They had the ball at the 5 yard line. They needed to go 95 yards for a winning score or 75 to move into field goal range.

Fouts completed a pass to the 28 yard line but John Jefferson failed to get out of bounds. The clock ticked – 36 seconds remaining – and Fouts threw the ball out of bounds to stop it. They moved the ball to the 41 with 10 seconds remaining. Mike Wood, the Charger kicker, was 0 for 3 from beyond 50 yards that season and San Diego knew it had to get closer.

We lined up and planned a four-man rush. We wanted to drop seven guys into coverage but still get pressure on Fouts, who stood in the shotgun. He snapped the ball, dropped back and scanned the coverage as the downfield play developed.

Our rush pushed the pocket back, closed the space and time in which Fouts had to throw, and he heaved it deep and into a crowd. I watched the ball float high in the air and the fans in the background became a blur. If a San Diego receiver caught the ball, the team would be well into field goal range. Perry, who appeared from nowhere, emerged from the group of players, jumped high into the air and tipped the ball. I watched as the ball hovered above the field, and six sets of hands reached up to grab it.

Perry somehow snatched the ball after tipping it, secured it and fell to the ground. This rookie, who played football in Canada and who failed to receive a look from anyone but us, had just grabbed his fourth interception of the day. All our players ran toward him, hugged and congratulated him. We had a lot of heroes this day, but none bigger than Vernon Perry.

"That's the greatest defensive game in the history of the NFL playoffs," Wade said. "Nobody has even come close to that."

Nielsen ran onto the field with 2 seconds remaining and ran the most beloved play in football: the kneel down. The final whistle sounded.

Perry jumped, twisted in mid-air with a teammate and threw his hands toward the sky. The defense we'd relied upon snagged five interceptions, and our wounded offense scored 17 points while committing only one turnover. Nobody but us believed we could do it.

"Once again, Bum ran up to me, threw his arms around me and said how proud he was of me," Nielsen said. "He told me when I retired from TV about six months ago – 30 years after that win – this was the greatest win he was ever a part of. I think it's the greatest win in Houston professional sports history."

"That was our finest hour," said Mauck, who took off his helmet after the game and waved it above his head in excitement. "We didn't have the talent they had but we plugged the gaps in the dyke. We got it done. We had adversity, and we didn't let it get us down."

So many kids who helped to beat San Diego became successful in football and in life. Harold Richardson, Mike Reinfeld and Ted Thompson became NFL general managers. Barber, Coleman, Nielsen and others became instrumental leaders of influential ministries. Mauck became a pro football coach. Dorris built a concrete business, sold it and retained a position within the company. Campbell launched a successful business, too. Ellender built a successful investment banking business. Burrough works in administration for his alma mater, Texas Southern University. Brazile and Carpenter dedicated their lives to coaching high school football, and Pastorini became president of a race car company.

"We never had any prima donnas," Burrough said. "Someone would have grabbed a guy like Terrell Owens around the neck and said, 'No way.'"

Brothers who live and work in unity tend to win. They also have fun. If your job isn't fun, you won't be real good at it to start with. I feel I had some influence on my players' outlooks and in their work habits. We convinced them you have to outwork your opponents, but we also taught them it's OK to have fun and to tell each other you love them.

BUM LESSON: Build a happy family by letting members be themselves.

It's important in business and in life to not only associate with good people, but to utilize them in ways that reflect their talents as well.

If people work for you, give them a chance to get better and let them do jobs they're capable of. Don't ask them to do something way over their head. Just like you build your offense or defense around the skill of the players on your team, you have to properly utilize the skills of those around you in other settings – and not force them to fit a mold you think they ought to.

Building a happy family often begins by letting members be who they are, and then spending the time it takes to make sure they know you care about them.

CHAPTER 10

WE HAD A WAY

"And we know that in all things God works for the good of those who love Him, who have been called according to his purpose." – Romans 8:28.

C oaching professional sports can often be a brutally unfair profession. All coaches understand this before they accept a job, but prior knowledge rarely dulls the sting of inevitability. Luckily for us, the Luv Ya Blue era blankets most of our disappointing memories.

"Like Daddy always said: 'There are two kinds of coaches,'" Wade said. "'Them that's been fired and them that's gonna be.' It's not always how well you do. Otherwise, he would still be coaching in Houston."

We had just defeated the San Diego Chargers at their home and advanced to the championship game – one step from appearing in the Super Bowl. We traveled to Pittsburgh once again to play the Steelers, the second consecutive year in which we faced Terry Bradshaw, Franco Harris and "Mean" Joe Greene in the championship game.

The first year we played Pittsburgh, the Steelers beat us 34-5. I'll never forget that loss or returning to Houston. We pulled into the Astrodome in team buses and more than

50,000 screaming, cheering fans awaited us. Our reception upon returning home after the second AFC Championship Game in Pittsburgh remains even more memorable. The fan loyalty is part of an era – dubbed Luv Ya Blue – the NFL has not enjoyed since.

Luv Ya Blue was a movement of dedicated Oilers fans who showed up to games singing fight songs and waving blue and white pom-poms. The movement caught fire in 1978 and continued into the next season. Never before had an NFL team's following created such excitement, devotion and colorful characters. Our games attracted the same type of passion the big-time college football programs enjoy. This excitement extended beyond the stadium, crept into almost every nook of Houston and expanded to other parts of the country. Our following, at least in terms of passion and loyalty, remains unparalleled even today.

"Luv Ya Blue was a phenomenon, unbelievable, exciting," Ronnie Coleman said. "Basically, it's a story about a bunch of guys and a coach who loved his city, loved his players and who loved the game. We were in the 1970s and just ahead of the racial divide of the 1960s. In Houston, Bum treated everybody the same, and I mean everybody. He basically brought a team and a town together."

Without the backing of Houstonians during the Luv Ya Blue period, I don't believe we would have reached the AFC Championship Game, let alone two years in a row. Those fans did as much to win close games as anything we did. If you had a football game without fans, you wouldn't have much of a ball game. Show me a silent group of fans and I'll show you a losing team. Our fans gave us an edge and pushed us to play better than we could otherwise. They let us know they loved us and appreciated what we did.

Fans get a lot of criticism; Philadelphia fans once booed Santa Claus. But fans were different in Houston. They liked our players not just because they played in the NFL, but because they could relate personally. Win or lose, our fans showed appreciation.

For perspective, I think it helps to remember the Oilers fell on hard times during the early 1970s. At the same time, the city experienced a population boom born out of petroleum industry job growth. Hard-working people of all sorts flocked to the city. By 1975, the year I became head coach, Houston was a melting pot with a bent toward cowboys. Our team just fit right in.

"The timing of the thing was just right," Wade said.

We had flashy guys such as Billy "White Shoes" Johnson and work horses such as Earl Campbell and Elvin Bethea. We had role players in Ronnie Coleman and Giff Nielsen, and wild and lively starters in Dan Pastorini and Kenny Burrough. Despite our differences, the city and the team found common ground, and we liked each other.

"I didn't have a pair of cowboy boots when I came down here from Utah," Nielsen said. "Now, I have six pair. I even have a pair of Luv Ya Blue boots. We had country western parties and rap parties. Bum was able to punch the right buttons for everyone. He was a legend because of how unique he was – the way he dressed, talked and coached. Wherever we went, people wanted to see Bum Phillips. They just couldn't believe a guy like him existed. He was Texas football. He broke down all the barriers on his team and then started to break down all the barriers of the city. I've never seen this in sports, and I don't think I ever will again. It's legendary."

You know you're on to something when Pastorini, who likes pretty girls and Ferraris, ditches his playboy clothes for western wear.

"This town and this team, it was Camelot, Shangri-La, all those imaginary things," Pastorini said.

The fans created an Oilers anthem, and the song became a bestseller in Houston. The chorus was "Houston Oilers No. 1." With hordes of new residents, a boom in the price of oil and a winning football team, pep rallies before and after games only served to heighten the sense we all lived in the same neighborhood and were in this together.

Isn't it funny how, just when it looks like you've found your place in life, everything changes in an instant? I know now God plants events in your life to move you in the direction He wants you to move. I would have benefited greatly from this understanding after the 1980 AFC Championship Game.

On Jan. 6, 1980, we again faced the Steelers fresh off a win in sunny San Diego. By the 1 p.m. kickoff the temperature in Three Rivers Stadium fell to a frigid 26 degrees, and 51,000 fans waved the Steelers' yellow "Terrible Towels."

Vernon Perry, our hero from the San Diego game a week before, gave us a glimmer of hope just minutes after the kickoff. He intercepted a Bradshaw pass and returned it 75 yards for a touchdown. Before the cold could even settle fully into our bones, we had a 7-0 lead.

We exchanged field goals before Bradshaw thawed. He then tossed two touchdown passes – one to John Stallworth – and propelled the Steelers to a 17-10 lead at halftime. What happened at the end of the third quarter spurred a change in how the NFL officiates games. A blown call led to the inclusion of instant replays in the game.

With just seconds remaining in the quarter, Pastorini dropped back from inside the Steelers' 10 yard line, threw a pass to Mike Renfro at the back of the endzone and scored a touchdown. The score would have tied the game going into the fourth quarter and given us much-needed momentum after a scoreless third quarter. The referees, though, said

Renfro failed to gather control of the ball before he stepped out of bounds. I still remember the famous NFL Films reel of Wade yelling at the call from the coach's box high in the stadium. It was clear to coaches, players and fans who watched the game on TV that Renfro caught the ball and fully established control in bounds. The ref's incomplete call, however, nullified the score, and we were forced to kick a field goal.

Pittsburgh went on to score 10 unanswered points and we lost 27-13.

Everybody says we would have won the game if the referees got the call right. I don't believe it. Pittsburgh was a better team than we were. The Steelers had better players. If we'd scored a touchdown, they would have found another way to beat us. The weather didn't beat us, and neither did the referees. The Steelers did. I do know this: If Pittsburgh hadn't made it to the AFC Championship Game two years in a row, we'd have defeated any other team that did.

"The first loss was devastating," Coleman said. "The second one we were in the game the whole time. By the second game, we were getting closer."

I couldn't believe we lost. For a man who became well-known for punchy post-game quotes, I was about as speechless as I've ever been. Art Rooney, the Steelers' owner, showed why his organization remains full of class and deserving of every good thing it gets.

About three minutes before the game ended, a large man – he must have stood about 6-foot-3-inches tall and weighed 270 pounds – walked right up to me from behind the players' benches.

"Mr. Rooney told me to escort you out of here," the man said.

When I walked after the final whistle through the crowd, it parted like the Red Sea. I mean *everybody* moved. I didn't know it at the time, but my escort was a famous Philadelphia boxer. Rooney wanted to make sure no fan stole the cowboy hat from atop my head like one did the year before. I left the stadium without as much as a breeze touching me.

"The Pittsburgh players had just as much class," Pastorini said. "We were walking off the field after that game and Dwight White and Joe Greene were on either side of me. They said, 'Man, you beat us.' I patted Joe Green on the face and told them to go win it for us. They didn't like playing us because they knew it was going to be a dogfight. We were going to war, but we all respected each other because of it."

Giff Nielsen didn't play in the second AFC Championship Game against Pittsburgh, but he helped us reach it. He also helped guys load the buses out in the cold, darkening parking lot. The sky dropped rain, and the freezing air turned it to slush. We'd lost and were ready to return home. We left Pittsburgh four hours later than planned, however, because of the worsening weather.

When we descended onto the Houston airport, we were beat up and beat down. It was late, and we were ready for one deep, off-season sleep. After departing the plane, we quickly boarded the team's buses. I told everyone we'd promised to show up at the Astrodome again, and the buses headed straight for it.

"We looked out the windows and saw people lining the streets, standing in their yards and waving at us as we rolled on," Nielsen said. "When we drove into the dome, it was more packed than it was the year before – and we'd lost again. That shows you the influence Bum had on the city. I've never seen anything like it."

I couldn't believe my eyes either. No fan base in this country would fill a stadium with 50,000 people after its team lost, and then return the next year after another loss and fill it with 80,000. I promise you there were 80,000 people in the stadium, and they probably broke a few hundred fire codes. Our fans were as proud of our football team as Pittsburgh fans were they won the game.

Our buses rolled onto the middle of the football field where organizers had already built a makeshift stage. Fans wanted to hear from every player. Mauck sang the National Anthem; Pastorini offered a fiery speech. Our disappointment turned to excitement.

"When they introduced Bum, it was pandemonium," Nielsen said.

Susan, my daughter, fought her way through the crowd to reach field level. She got close enough to the stage to see my watery eyes.

I didn't know what I was going to say, but I knew darned well those fans didn't want to hear we would try harder the next time. Those people had been sitting there for six hours, and they wanted to hear something to pep them up. An idea struck me seconds before I grabbed the microphone.

"Last year we knocked on the door," I said, the beginning of an uproar rising within the fans.

"This year we beat on it," I continued.

"Next year we're going to kick the son of a bitch in."

I've never heard a roar quite like I did at that moment – not before and never since. In recent years, NFL Films voted me the league's No. 8 Character of All Time. It's too bad the distinction didn't include our players and fans. Together, we created the greatest connection between a team and a town the league might ever know.

"That was the most emotional thing I've ever been a part of," Wade said. "I still get the chills thinking about it."

We worked hard the next season to fulfill the vow we made to the fans inside the Astrodome, despite starting the year on the wrong foot. The year before, Pastorini asked to be traded.

"You give me another year, and if you still want to be traded, I'll trade you," I told my quarterback.

After we lost to Pittsburgh the second time, Pastorini approached me again.

"Maybe it was time for a change. I'd started believing everybody – that I wasn't good enough," Pastorini said. "I was taking Novocain to heal the pain from the last six games of the previous year. I'd lost my throwing motion and arm strength. When we lost the second AFC Championship Game, it was the low point of my life."

Pastorini asked to be traded and I granted it. Next to the mistake I made cutting the high school boy for missing track practice, releasing Pastorini was the second biggest error of my career. I should have kept my mouth shut. We were both foolish.

Despite losing Pastorini to Oakland, we amassed an 11-5 record and entered the playoffs as a Wild Card team. Thanks to a 1,934-yard season from Earl Campbell – who earned Offensive Player of the Year honors – we looked like a team still poised for greatness. Irony has a funny of way of ending things on its terms, though. We were forced to play a road playoff game in Oakland.

We lost the game 27-7 and Tom Flores, the Raiders head coach, led Oakland to the big game. For the third year in a row, we lost in the playoffs to the eventual Super Bowl winner.

Unfortunately, our team owner, Bud Adams, fired me after the Oakland loss. I have a hunch about why he fired me, but it's probably unfair for me to give my one-sided opinion here. Suffice it to say part of his decision centered on the idea it was wrong for me to get too close to my players. Adams thought a more disciplined approach would get us over the hump.

The day they fired me in Houston is still referred to in the city as the New Year's Eve massacre. Houston was my home and, boy, I thought I had everything in life I wanted, but the next moment it was gone. We had a good thing going, and I had as good a coaching record as anyone.

"I played until the year after Bum was fired," Coleman said. "It was like having a good wife, divorcing her and going to a bad wife. That's all I'm going to say about that."

The day I was fired, I didn't immediately tell anyone the news. Susan, my daughter, watched TV and gasped when she saw a scrolling news flash at the bottom of the screen: "Bum Phillips was just fired by the Houston Oilers."

She tried calling my office, but all she got was a busy signal. A rush of incoming calls tied up most of the lines. She tried Wade's private line, but to no avail.

Finally, she called my house and her mother said I was by myself out at the new home we were building.

"When I walked up behind him, of course he was crying," Susan said. "He didn't want me to feel bad, so he told me, smiling, 'I just lost my job. I'm not dying.'"

Susan and I just sat there, silent. She left when players started arriving. She said hi to Mauck and hugged me goodbye. She knew the silence would soon be replaced by rough talk, and she wanted to give me time to vent.

I had no idea Adams would fire me, and I declined media interviews until I could gather my thoughts. The next day, I called a press conference.

I told reporters the same thing I told my children: As the owner, he had every right to let me go – and I'll never say a bad word about him. For years, the media tried to lure me into insulting Adams, but I never did. Just as I looked forward after the war, I set my sights on my future.

Well, I found another job within two days of being fired and was lucky enough to go to work for John Mecom and the New Orleans Saints.

"Bum was too big a hero in Bud Adams' eyes," Mecom, the former Saints owner, said. "Bum was also a hero in New Orleans, even before I hired him. That was unusual. It was difficult for people in New Orleans to accept Texans."

We became good friends because we shared the same passions: football and creating football families.

The year after I left Houston, the Oilers went 7-9. The team then went 1-8 during a strike year, 2-14, 3-13 and then 5-11. The Oilers didn't win more than five games until 1987. I don't say this because I'm happy they lost. I just can't help but think the sudden decline shows the way we did it there just worked.

Houston's football team moved to Tennessee in 1997 and now the Oilers only live in our memories.

Tom Danyluk wrote a great book, "The Super 70s." In it, he said some really nice things about me.

"The problem with coaches who are blessed with a quick wit is that they are usually remembered for what they said in the papers rather than what their teams did on the field," Danyluk wrote. "Bum Phillips was the best known 'funny' coach of pro football in the 1970s, part one-liner, part two-a-day. But what was no joke was Phillips' ability to coach the game of football and motivate the boys who played for him."

While I appreciate Danyluk's words, we struggled in New Orleans just as the Oilers did when I left. We never recaptured the Luv Ya Blue phenomenon in Louisiana because you couldn't bottle it and move it anywhere. Our best year was in 1983 when we went 8-8. I retired in 1985 never having reached the playoffs but for the magical time I spent in Houston.

When Luv Ya Blue died, so did a memorable era enjoyed by many people.

"Bum was one of the last real romantics left in professional sports," Mecom, the former Saints owner, said. "Bum is the reason I stayed in pro football as long as I did. I don't care if he's a year younger than me, he became a father figure. I don't know if he doesn't want to show it or he expects you to understand it, but his IQ is exceptionally high. Houston's decision to let him go wasn't so smart."

I live in Goliad, Texas, these days, but I returned to Houston on Oct. 4, 2009, as I do from time to time. My second wife, Debbie, and I were in town to attend a Houston Texans game.

By midmorning this Sunday, we drove straight to Reliant Stadium. Because we were guests of team owner Bob McNair, a wealthy Houston businessman, we drove right onto the ramp that takes players, coaches and game officials to an area beneath the stadium. We parked near the visiting team's buses, visited with a few police officers and stadium staff and were then chaperoned on an eight-seat golf cart into a series of wide hallways.

Debbie was there as an honorary team captain to promote Breast Cancer Awareness Month. She survived the cancer and was one of a select few chosen to stand on the field before kickoff as part of a league-wide effort to help find a cure. During that month, many of the players wore pink – pink gloves, shoes or ribbons – during games to show support. I was there to support Debbie, to sign autographs, do radio and TV interviews and to help promote the Texans and Bum's Smokehouse, our in-stadium eatery.

After a long golf cart ride, and a short walk down another hallway, they escorted us into a special section of the stadium. A Houston Texans TV crew interviewed me within minutes.

"I always love returning to Houston," I told the reporter. "I'd still be coaching if Bob McNair owned the team when I left the NFL. It's a new team now, but it's still Houston. In the end, the city makes the team. I don't guess I've mentally left. I still love this city."

I sat on a bench, drank bottled water and prepared for a live radio show set to broadcast outside and near the fans who gathered before the game.

Then, of all people to approach me, Tom Flores came up and shook my hand. The Raiders were in town to play the Texans, and Flores is Oakland's game day radio show host. We said hello and visited for a few moments.

Flores, you might remember, coached the Raiders during the last game I ever coached in Houston – the 1980 playoff game we lost. It was good see him, anyhow, and equally good to see he's doing well.

As we waited for the live radio show hosts to usher us outside, a few former players stopped by to say hi. Zeke Moore, a former offensive tackle, and Charlie Frazier, a former Pro Bowl wide receiver, gave me a big hug and we caught up briefly. Both men are now Texans ambassadors and work to promote the team. Before long, our stadium escorts led us to an outdoor plaza where Sports Radio 610 had built a tarpaulin-covered pavilion to stay dry amid a gray, drizzly morning.

We laughed and joked and talked about the promise the young Texans team showed.

"I like where I'm at now," I said into the radio station's microphone. "No matter how long I live, Houston will always be No. 1, though."

After the radio show, I stood at the foot of the covered stage and signed autographs. Despite the drizzle, diehard Luv Ya Blue fans held out footballs, clothing and photos. One man, a 46-year-old named Ralph, wore a Houston Oilers jacket.

"Bum was my idol," he said. "I've had that jacket forever. To this day, I get excited about Bum and the Houston Oilers."

We were then whisked back inside, into an elevator, along a concourse, into another glass-encased elevator and finally to a spot outside Bum's Smokehouse. There, organizers positioned two tables so I could sit and sign autographs. Kimann, my daughter, sat next to me while Debbie offered interviews to Fox Sports Southwest.

"Thank you for doing this," one woman, who stood in the long line, told me. She pointed down the line to a man. "You made my husband a little kid again. Look at him grinning."

She smiled and we had a good laugh. It felt great to be up close and personal with the fans again.

What struck me was the mix of people who waited for an autograph: people of all races, young and old, male and female. The clothes they wore ranged from cutoff shorts and dress slacks to Texans jerseys and old Oilers jerseys.

A man named Frank wore a sombrero. He said he was born in 1974 and thus was too young to understand football by the time we took the reigns in Houston. But he was in the Astrodome with his father following the playoff losses to Pittsburgh at the end of the 1978 and 1979 seasons. This 35-year-old was there as a boy to greet us in the old stadium and was here this day to do the same as a man.

"Bum was different, a cowboy through and through. He's one of us," Frank said. "I know people who talk like him, act like him."

Kimann sat next to me and smiled from ear to ear as fans shared stories. As a young girl, she often stood behind me during autograph sessions. It was nice to have her at my side this time.

Fans brought all sorts of memorabilia – Luv Ya Blue scarves, shirts, hats and cheering cones – and everything in between. One woman brought a "Go Blue!" foam finger, which had faded badly because she'd bought it 30 years before. The most popular item fans had me sign was a photograph of me waving at the crowd during a Luv Ya Blue reunion at Reliant Stadium just a few years before.

"Thank you for the wonderful memories," the woman with the foam finger said.

"Bum was the most humorous coach I ever saw. He was a lively cuss," said a 60-year-old named Bob. "He got the most out of every player. He was just a down-to-Earth, country-fried gentleman. Everybody in this city who liked football liked Bum Phillips."

Debbie, Kimann and her husband, Mark, joined me in Bob and Janice McNair's owner's suite during the game. Former U.S. Secretary of State James Baker sat behind us. The long luxury suite is filled with 20 flat-screen TVs, Texans and Oilers memorabilia, helmets, footballs and player posters. The food served – quail wrapped in bacon, filet mignon, foreign cheeses and more – could have easily been straight out of a four-star restaurant.

The Texans beat the Raiders 29-6. The day proved to be a homecoming of sorts I won't soon forget.

While I couldn't help but think briefly about being fired in Houston 30 years before, I was reminded again things work out the way they do for a reason. I love Houston, but after football I found myself surrounded by passions of a different kind: the love of a woman, ranching and the life you can only have once you devote yours to God.

BUM LESSON: Don't dwell on the past, especially if it includes disappointments.

I think we can all agree bad things happen to good people. Coaches get fired, people divorce and economies crash.

How you respond to hurdles – and whether you choose to dwell on disappointment or focus positively on the future – determines the level of success and happiness you achieve in life.

I chose to take what I learned during World War II and use it to make myself and others better. Except for the purposes of this book, I have not once dwelled on the atrocities I witnessed. Was it fair young men and friends died? No. But it does neither them nor me any good to allow this regrettable reality to steal my happiness today.

Was it fair Bud Adams fired me? Probably not. But not once did I allow his decision to hinder my work with the Saints, as a businessman and now as a rancher.

We all incur disappointments in life – some bigger than others. You honor God by giving Him your worries and bad memories, and by refocusing your thoughts on the promising future He paves for you.

CHAPTER 11

THE RETIREMENT WAY

*"Have I not commanded you? Be strong and courageous.
Do not be terrified; do not be discouraged, for the Lord your
God will be with you wherever you go." – Joshua 1:9.*

I never took anything in life I didn't earn. That's why I wrote "Void" on all the pages of my New Orleans head coaching contract, left $1.3 million on the table and said goodbye to football in 1985 for full-time work on my ranch. I was proud of what I'd done and was ready to move on. I left on my terms.

To be honest, I wasn't quite sure how I'd spend all my time. I bought about 750 head of mama cows, lived just outside Houston and leased 5,000 acres. I went to work at 62 years old as a rancher, returning as an older man to the passion I developed as a youngster in Orange.

While my children and I disagree, my transition from the hectic demands of the National Football League to life as a private rancher was easy. I coached football for decades and then simply settled into a new job. My children offer a more complicated assessment.

Ranching, you remember, was always part of my life. Football only replaced it for awhile. I love being around cattle, horses and people. I don't like to brag on myself, but I had plenty of money and endorsement opportunities, a great home and a ranch to call my own. Life was good.

During the next few years, though, I divorced, married a strong-headed woman and left life in Houston behind for a quieter, more rural one. God knows how to reveal certain truths just about the time you're ready to accept them.

I'm not at all excited to discuss publicly my divorce from Helen. We were married 44 years and had six great children. Some things ought to stay between a man and a woman, and the cause of divorce is certainly one of them. I know full well, though, I can't discuss my Christian journey without offering an honest explanation of why I broke one of the faith's most taboo doctrines. Because this is a touchy subject, all I'll say is our split wasn't Helen's fault, and it wasn't my fault. We'd grown apart to the point we barely had a relationship. Divorce is rarely good. Now that Debbie and I are believers and growing in faith daily, we wish divorce never was a part of our lives, but we also know we are together for a reason. We love an old bumper sticker: "Christians aren't perfect, just forgiven." We're far from perfect, but we've asked for forgiveness. God continues to use us just as Jesus used imperfect people. Falling in love wasn't the Christian thing to do, but we're happy God brought us together when we needed each other most.

After football, I felt content to spend my days in the barn or working cattle. I stayed busy in business, too. My daughter Kimann, though, said she witnessed a struggle brewing within me.

"He had a lot of things going on, but he didn't know who he was," she said. "He didn't get up in the morning and go to work on a football field somewhere. No longer did all the decisions – from the play calls to the roster and the paint color in his office – come from him. He found himself sitting in a house wondering what good he could do. He had a routine for almost 50 years, and then suddenly he had none. He won't tell you this, but he was searching for what makes him happy. He was searching for Jesus, and he didn't even know it."

I never really thought about it too much until I heard her say those words, but she's probably correct. I was searching for something, and God delivered in a big way. He steered a woman named Debbie into my life. Without her, I might have stayed on the Houston ranch, worked cattle and avoided church like a ranch dog dodges his weekly bath.

After Kimann earned her degree in 1989 – she was the last of my children to graduate from college – I walked into her bedroom one morning. All my kids were on their way in life and so, too, was the baby of the family. I walked to Kimann's bed, put my hand on her shoulder and woke her. I let her rub the sleep from her eyes, told her I loved her and said after a few moments I planned to divorce her mother.

Kimann took our divorce hard, but she understands the dynamics better today.

"My mother still loves Dad and still tells her children and grandchildren positive stories about him," Kimann said. "Football can create stress and strain because it took so much of his time. There were decades of moving and working through high school, college and the NFL. Without God as the connecting factor, they drifted apart."

Because of football, we took only one vacation – in 1964. My marriage began to suffer as far back as my high school coaching days in Nederland.

When I met Debbie, she was married to a Houston dentist. I knew her husband and son, a local TV sports anchor who covered the Oilers. We often attended the same parties and events, but for a long time remained passing acquaintances.

We shared a passion for horses, though, and we occasionally bumped into each other at cutting horse events. One time, Debbie helped during a clinic, and I was there as one of the students.

"The first time I really remember being around Bum enough to talk to him was during the Jim Reno-Shorty Freeman cutting horse clinic," Debbie said. "I was a great fan and a great admirer. He was Bum Phillips and I was a 'hey-you.' I admired him and respected him, but I wasn't star struck."

Debbie is a special kind of woman. She's beautiful and tough, organized and driven. She grew up an only child and because her parents also moved often, she formed into a bit of a loner who preferred the company of adults over friendships with students her own age. Our 26-year age difference never bothered either one of us.

My former players care for Debbie as if she's their mother.

"Bum taught me how to love," said Kenny Burrough, our standout receiver in Houston. "Well, I love him and I'm just as close to his wife. If she didn't love Bum, I wouldn't like Debbie. I call her all the time. We respect Debbie. Notice I said 'we.' Nobody's going to mess with Debbie, and anybody from the Oilers would agree."

Debbie was born in Fort Worth and comes from a long line of accountants and bookkeepers. Early on, though, she developed a passion for horses. As a baby, she was colicky and her parents took her to ride the Shetland ponies – the only remedy they could find to quell her crying. Growing up, she lived in the city but always had a horse stowed away on a nearby lot or at a family ranch in the country. When she left home, she maintained two jobs: one to feed her and another to support her horses.

Debbie graduated Suma Cum Laude from her high school, and she turned her smarts into a business. She broke rowdy colts for paying customers and entered into the sport of cutting horses as a professional.

In the old days, ranchers didn't have fences and cattle pens. Everybody's cattle ran together. When ranchers herded 3,000 head of cattle, they singled their cows out and then roped, threw and branded them. The cowboys rode atop the best horses and "cut" the calves out of the herd to brand them. Then, one day, they made this job into a high-paying contest you might have seen on TV. The contests challenge riders to cut cows from a herd and to keep them from the others for about two-and-a-half minutes. The lone cow, of course, wants badly to rejoin the herd. When it veers left, your horse must, too. If the cow veers right, same thing. Judges watch to see if your horse stays in sync with the cow. To watch a horse do this in deep sand inside a rodeo arena is some sight, let me tell you. And so was Debbie. She competed across the United States, earned quite a bit of money and reached the World Finals. She worked her way up the ranks to become one of the nation's Top 10 competitors and earned the No. 8 spot one year. At major aged events she vied against 600 other entrants, including men, and routinely made the finals.

During the summer of 1986, Debbie worked a yearling colt and it reared up and pawed her in the face. The colt knocked Debbie to the barn floor, crushed her nose and forced it to the side of her cheek. When she regained consciousness, she reached for her face, which was numb. She walked to her house, up the porch steps and banged on the door. A woman inside, who worked for her, saw Debbie's bloodied face and immediately ran for towels. Debbie removed the towels once she reached the bathroom.

"You have no idea how bizarre you look when you have no nose," Debbie said. "When I stood in the mirror and saw myself for the first time, I was pretty shocked."

My trainer, Nolan Powell, told me about Debbie, who was bedridden with two black eyes, stitches and the sting of broken bones. When I went to see if she was OK, all I saw was a towel, filled with ice cubes, wrapped around her face.

She suffered the injuries on a Thursday, and doctors scheduled surgery for late the following week. On the Monday before surgery, she returned to work her horses and then called the doctor. She asked to reschedule the surgery, despite the temporary facial deformities, so she could compete in an upcoming show.

"I'm not your typical female," Debbie said, laughing. "I've always been a tomboy, always been comfortable in a man's world. Let's just say I didn't spend a lot of time in front of a mirror during those first few days, though. My nose was huge."

After I retired, we worked together more often and started to get to know each other. We both loved horses, people and football. We didn't set out to fall in love; it just happened. While we fell in love before we were both divorced, neither of us really had marriages. I'm not defending our courtship, but I'm glad we had it. We're both positive, forward-looking people and we didn't know so much happiness existed until we fell in love.

We've been married 20 years now, spend 24 hours a day together and we've never had one fight. We've had disagreements, of course, but she wins every single one of them.

Debbie was saved in 1982, the year she gave her life to Christ. She'd always been a seeker, even in high school. By the time we married, she was well along a spiritual walk that began almost 10 years before. If you compare our walks to journeys through school, she was in college, and I sat at the back of the first-grade classroom.

"When Bum and I realized we cared more for each other than just friends, I made Bum go meet Gussie, my Bible study teacher," Debbie said.

Debbie had been going to see Gussie for some time. My wife always knew God existed, but she didn't always find Him in churches. She found the Lord in Gussie's house, though. Gussie could talk to you about the Bible in a way you could understand it. I enjoyed her Bible study sessions and I remember the first time Debbie prompted me to go.

"Bum didn't know Christ or that he needed Him," Debbie said. "When we first realized we were in love, I told him because of where I was in my walk with the Lord, there'd be no relationship with me unless I was his wife. He was OK with that."

Gussie was a school teacher who, in her home, taught Bible study classes for many of the city's well-known women. She had soft eyes, chiseled cheekbones and gray hair. The first Bible study class I attended was in her living room, and she studied me as if Debbie brought home a boyfriend she shouldn't have.

Gussie had cookies, coffee and a card table she positioned nearby. She sat behind the table, read one chapter from the Bible and then explained what it meant. I studied the beige carpet, the aging furniture, the all-white walls and every word Gussie spoke. After an hour, some visitors left and some lingered. Debbie always took notes and recorded each session. She played the recordings in my truck anytime we took a ride.

"A marriage between a believer and a non-believer won't work," Debbie said. "I loved Bum enough to marry him, but at every possible moment when we were in the car traveling, I'd have a Gussie tape in. You can't make anyone accept Christ as your savior. I just tried to plant the seed every chance I got. 'Do you mind if I listen to a Gussie tape?' I'd ask. For the first years, he intentionally read or interrupted and talked about something else. I'd just turn it off and have the conversation. As soon as he was through, I'd turn it back on."

This was the first time I really thought about the Bible because I'd always taken the book for granted. To be honest, I thought Jesus and God were the same. I know they're the same, in essence, but I didn't know you need to go through Jesus to get to God. The more you learn, the more you examine your life, decisions and behaviors.

"God changed our focus from 'me, me, me and what I want' to each other," Debbie said. "When you start living a Christ-like life, you take the focus off your needs, desires and wants and put it on others' needs, wants and desires. Bum likes to joke we don't argue because he acquiesces to what I say. When it boils down to it, he's the head of household and his decision is final. In my younger days, before I had God in my life, I'd go to the extreme – my way or the highway."

How has Debbie been as a wife? Best one I got. I say this with a wink and a smile for the woman who helped me to find Christ. Our relationship today is stronger than it was 20 years ago, and we thank God for that. She knows me well enough to know if I screw up, she can tell me about it – and it goes both ways. We have no ulterior motives, we say what we mean and accept each other. You can understand why I became nervous when I thought I might lose her to cancer.

Debbie never had a lazy bone in her body, so it's ironic, I suppose, her body began to fail her. Debbie first had uterine cancer in 1983, but she survived and went into remission. Six months after we married, doctors diagnosed her with breast cancer. During the next few years, she endured other heart-wrenching news: Her father, Gussie and two close friends died of cancer.

"There was so much joy in my marriage with Bum, but there were joys and there were sorrows," Debbie said. "I was blessed to have a very slow-growing type of cancer."

Doctors didn't think Debbie's cancer would respond well to chemotherapy, so they put her on debilitating medicine and removed both her breasts. Two weeks after surgery, she was cleaning the stove and moving just fine. A week later, after starting her medicine, she was so sick she couldn't get out of bed. Being the stubborn woman she is, she stopped taking the medicine. It's tough enough for a woman to lose both breasts, but Debbie was even angrier she couldn't work.

"The biggest blessing was that it wasn't a big deal to Bum that I lost both breasts," Debbie said. "I tried for a while to wear breast prosthetics, but that didn't last long. They were so hot and heavy and uncomfortable. We were at this charity golf tournament in Houston – at the farthest point from the clubhouse on the course. Well, I swung at the golf ball and my falsie popped out. I had to cross my arms over my chest or it would have fallen out the bottom of my shirt. There was a nearby grove of trees and I went there to put them back in place. I decided never to wear them again."

Doctors have tested Debbie every year since she went off her medication, and so far the cancer remains in remission. She saw her friends and family endure painful treatments, and none worked. She believes early detection is the key, and thus is an avid supporter of the Susan G. Komen Foundation, a Dallas-based group dedicated to educating women and researching breast cancer's causes and treatments. She knows firsthand how cancer can change lives.

"I went through some pretty serious depressions, especially after losing Daddy, Gussie and when Cissy, my close friend, was diagnosed," Debbie said. "I think of that as my time in the wilderness. It's a period of time where you learn true obedience, true submission to God and His

Will, true trust and dependence on Him. God doesn't let you become a witness until He molds you into a trustworthy witness."

As I've mentioned, Debbie stood as a witness to faith – and at the 50 yard line – inside Reliant Stadium before the October 2009 Houston Texans-Oakland Raiders game. She is a cancer survivor, and she stood with a select few other survivors as honorary team captains to promote Breast Cancer Awareness Month. Players from both teams stood on the sidelines, TV cameras zeroed in on the field and fans cheered when they saw those ladies on the big screen.

God tested Debbie during her rough stretch to prepare her for the work He'd soon call her to do. As for me, I know God reveals certain truths just about the time you're ready to accept them. I had no idea after moving to Goliad He'd reveal Himself to me inside a prison.

BUM LESSON: When you need God, He finds you.

I fear too many families believe in God but fail to fully seek Him for their lives. Just as I did for so long, many people take God and heaven for granted.

When you realize you need God, though, He comes through for you in a big way.

For me, retirement, divorce and Debbie's battle with cancer were challenges that should have made me seek God, although I still did not know it at the time.

While I continued to take baby steps of faith, my family found itself well along a walk with the Lord. In differing ways, Debbie and my children advanced their understanding and appreciation of God's Word. They gravitated toward, helped and encouraged each other.

"With Dad being in his seventies, how blessed we are God revealed Himself and brought us together at about the same time," Dee Jean said.

If you need God, you will find Him. Sometimes it takes tragedy and disappointment, but it doesn't have to. No matter what your experience, ask for Him to come into your life, and He will.

You can say, in football terms, that for a long time I fumbled the ball when it came to seeking the Lord. The good news is God recovered it for me, as Debbie reminds me.

Matthew 7:7 reminds us: "Ask and it will be given to you; seek and you will find; knock and the door will be opened to you."

CHAPTER 12

THE PRISON WAY

"I needed clothes and you clothed me, I was sick and you looked after me, I was in prison and you came to visit me." – Matthew 25:36

Debbie and I love Houston, but we yearned to enjoy a less hectic and more rural setting. For years we sought land where we could build a ranch; a homestead we'd settle upon for good to pursue the way of life we'd both always known and loved.

Houston's growth began to constrict our small ranch on the city's outskirts, and the demands of the celebrity lifestyle became too much. I don't resent the time we spent doing charitable work, seminars or endorsements. If someone asked for help, we offered it. But we reached the point we could barely keep up with all the requests. When developers began work on a 12-lane highway outside our front door, traffic only pushed us faster toward quieter pastures.

Debbie and I looked everywhere – south near Kingsville, north outside Kerrville and the Texas Hill Country, and every stop along the way. We looked at grassy pastures, rocky outcrops and at prices that spanned the spectrum. Nothing we toured fully fit our wants. The ones we liked we couldn't afford, and the ones we could afford we didn't like. We finally spotted a newspaper ad, which highlighted land for sale in Beeville, a quiet town in South Texas. We traveled several times to inspect properties and stopped during return trips to eat in the county just north of Beeville. In these parts, everybody knows everybody and we fit right in with the characters from nearby Goliad County.

As luck would have it, our Beeville Realtor said a ranch, which was not yet on the market, might be just what we were looking for.

"Would you mind being in Goliad County?" she asked.

"Not at all," we told her.

We drove along a winding road, up and down hills that open to vast green, flowing pastures and alongside a mix of brush, trees and spacious, scenic valleys. We turned off the highway, traveled along a paved county road for about a mile and turned to our right. From the turnoff, we could barely see the 250-acre property. Dense brush, which choked 80 percent of the land here, blocked our view. Slowly, we cruised up the half-mile private, paved driveway, around a tall oak tree and to the front of the house. We felt lost in a sea of solid brush and trees, but we loved it. The house was OK – engulfed in Austin white stone, which we both like – and the land was otherwise largely undeveloped: no barn, stables or cutting arena. The property had only a perimeter fence and half the cattle pens it does now. We knew going in it would be a lot of work. We visited the following week and rode the property on horseback, squeezing between the tall, thick brush while on the lookout for rattlesnakes in the grass. While riding from the front of the land to the farthest corner, we decided we'd found our dream property.

As it turns out, the seller's great-grandparents settled in the original Stephen F. Austin colony near Houston, and then on this land in 1826, about a decade before Texas became a state. The land and home stayed with one family for almost 200 years.

We signed the deal on the hood of our Suburban in nearby Goliad, and the homestead became our own. We are only the second family in Texas history to claim it.

The seller was kind enough to share her "IO" brand and a story we love to tell. Her great grandfather won the land about 130 years ago in a card game and thus branded his cattle with "IO" – which is short for "I owe" – to gig the loser, who was his cousin.

This area, much like Orange, was settled by gunfighters, regulators and vigilantes. Goliad County also once boasted a famous hanging tree at the town square. The county is home to the Presidio La Bahia, a landmark to a time when the Spaniards occupied it. Goliad earned its name in 1829 and is the phonetic anagram of Hidalgo, a hero and priest during the Mexican Revolution.

On moving day, May 27, 1995, seven trucks pulling 30-foot cattle trailers rumbled down the road from our home outside Houston, down historic U.S. Highway 59, along the narrow county road and atop our new, paved driveway. We'd loaded fence posts and boards, horses and cattle, clothes and pans.

The night we moved in, the skies opened up. It rained 2.5 inches the first night and not again until September 1996.

Because the property lacked landscaping and other buildings we'd need to work cattle and horses, we set out immediately to put our stamp on the IO Ranch. Friends must have thought we'd lost our minds. I don't think they saw the diamond in the rough.

During the next few years, we planted thousands of posts, built riding pens, barns and added special wire to the perimeter to keep out rooting feral hogs. Using skills I learned on a bulldozer in the military, I cleared 95 percent of the brush and saved the prettier trees for scenery and cattle shade. We built the Debbie Dome, a covered arena that shades Debbie from the unforgiving Texas sun while she works our cutting horses.

The property blossomed into what we knew it could become. Friends who'd thought we were crazy finally saw the place for the beauty it held. I just hope everyone in the world can be as happy in the latter part of life as I am in mine.

We turned the rough country into a welcome home for friends and family. Former players visit often, and when we were a bit younger, singers and songwriters did, too. We once invited two dozen friends to our home, and we sat around, picked and grinned. The bunch included country songwriters Sonny Throckmorton and Casey Kelly, writers of George Strait's "Cowboy Rides Away;" Rock Killough, Craig Dillingham and others who call the Country Music Hall of Fame home. The Beatles opened for Bruce Channel when he toured Europe with his smash hit "Hey, Baby," and he played for us on our Goliad ranch. These are good folks, deep folks, and we love to be around them.

Although the nearest neighbor is a mile away, I'm certain he sat outside and enjoyed the free concerts played right here on my favorite land.

I know a lot about football, ranching and barbecue, but during this period I still wasn't up to speed on spirituality. Lord knows I'd carved out a piece of His Earth, and it offered its own sort of spirituality. I knew the rules of the land and the tricks to spread the right type of grass seed from one side of the road to the other. For some reason, though, I still struggled to take an important step in my own path down the road to salvation.

One day a few years after we moved in, I received an interesting phone call from Mike Barber, our former tight end in Houston. I hadn't heard from him in years.

Barber had a violent temper when he played football for me and for good reason. He was well-behaved, though, the first time we met.

"We were in his office the day after the draft, and I was just in awe," Barber said. "I was nervous and didn't know what to expect. Walking in there, he was so kind, easy-going and relaxed. It didn't take about two or three minutes for me to relax. He shared his heart and what he expected of me. Like I say, he has one son, but he has a ton of kids."

Barber came to me as a troubled young man. Football was his escape from a depressing home life. When he was younger, Barber's father cursed him out from the sideline, belittled him in front of others and beat him behind closed doors.

"Dad was a painter by trade," Barber said. "We lived from shoestring to shoestring. For years and years and years, our furniture was cardboard boxes, and he painted for rent."

Chaos loomed inside my former tight end's home. His dad beat him hard and with anything handy. His mother lost her hair four or five times because of the stress.

"The last time he hit me was with a hammer in the head," Barber said. "I was able to get up, stagger back to the bedroom and to get there just in time to lock it. I saw it in the corner – a bat. I walked out of the room and said, 'You ever hit me again, you're going to have to kill me.'"

Barber's dad abused his boy in ways that festered when the son entered college. One day after a college practice, a coach cussed at him and Barber sprinted 500 yards to the field house, tossed off his shoulder pads and hopped in his car. He drove two and half hours to find his dad.

"Dad, I'm sorry, and I love you," Barber told his dad when he finally found him. His dad didn't say a word in response, but a portion of the weight holding Barber down suddenly lifted.

"Deep inside he knew what he had done, but I had to forgive him," Barber said. "Later in life, we had some good talks, and I told him about Christ. He was in the hospital and could barely talk, but he gave his life to Jesus. He died in 1986 and I celebrated his funeral. I had joy. I knew where he was headed."

When Barber joined the Oilers, he was talented but a bit emotionally fragile. One day during his rookie year, I stood atop the coach's tower. From my perch, I saw him mess up big time on a play. Instead of yelling, I climbed down the ladder and walked straight up to him. With my thumb and index finger, I gently grabbed a piece of his jersey.

"I'm not much of a coach if I can't get the athletic ability out of you, son," I said, turning and returning to my tower.

"That was one pivotal moment," Barber said. "The things I'd been through, where I was at in my life … It was a gesture that said, 'I believe in you. I'm honored to have you as one of my players.' It gave me such a lift. It helped me to realize I do belong here. At that moment, I looked at Coach Phillips like he was my father, and that look has never changed."

After football, Barber devoted himself to full-time prison ministry. One day, he explained why he hadn't called in years.

"I can't tell you how many times I wanted to pick up the phone and call," Barber said. "I knew coach believed in me, but I didn't know if he believed in what I was doing – the prison ministry. I love to talk about God. I didn't want to make him feel uncomfortable. If there's a guy sitting there with a beer bottle in his hand, in my mind, he isn't going to want to talk about God. Out of respect, I left him alone."

Similarly, Barber avoided his teammates. Then, one day he watched an ESPN special about me, our team and the Luv Ya Blue days. The show served as the kick in the pants he needed to call.

"Hey, Coach. No. 86," Barber said.

"Hey, boy. You've been on my mind," I told him, and we talked for awhile.

"What are the chances of you coming into prison with me?" he said.

"I want to go. I've been waiting for you to ask me."

After a nice talk, Barber said he wanted to visit and take me to a place not far from my ranch. He wanted take me to a prison in Beeville, a small town about a half-hour south and down the road. I was all for seeing Barber again and joining him on a trip he said was important.

I climbed into the SUV, Barber sat up front and another fella drove. After a short while, Barber turned from the front passenger seat, put his hand on a Bible he'd set on the center console and asked me if I'd given my life to Jesus Christ. I was so surprised, I lied. The God part I was already up on. Jesus Christ was a different story. I told Barber, yes, I'd already given my life to Jesus – even though I hadn't.

Barber ministered to inmates in the prison – which he's done now for decades – and I spoke some, too. The experience of seeing those kids who were locked up warm to our visit and share stories about how they got there did something to me I never expected. The trip moved me so much I visited another prison a month later. After we talked to those inmates, we left in a white van. I told Barber about my lie and said I've always thought being a good ol' boy was enough to make it to heaven.

"Coach," Barber said, "I can remember you telling me it doesn't matter what kind of player I was in college. Without the playbook I wasn't stepping on your field. You see this Bible? That's your new playbook. You have to use this to make Jesus the Lord of your life."

"Well, I want to go to heaven," I said. "How do I do that?"

Barber looked at me and prayed. I closed my eyes and joined him. I asked Jesus to be the Lord of my life.

"That's it?" I said.

"Did you mean that with all of your heart?" Barber asked.

"Of course I did."

"Well, Coach, you don't say anything you don't mean. You had a number of rules for us during training camp and we all knew to go by them – or else. That's the way God is. He loves us like you love your players, but you have to play the game by His rules to get in."

I leaned back in the seat and threw my hands up. I finally understood it. Believing in the system means obeying the system, and I was given a game plan. I thought about my decisions during retirement and then leaned forward.

"Can a beer drinker make it to heaven?" I asked.

"Let me put it this way," Barber said. "You want to be an All-Pro for God or just a regular player?"

"I want to be an All-Pro."

I'd waited 76 years, but I'd finally accepted my Savior. I'd like to think I've always tried to be a good person and live by the Golden Rule. During the next few years, though, I witnessed and learned all new things about life. This, of course, is just the beginning of that story.

Like most Saturdays, our front door swung open and shut. Visitors – a neighbor from down the road or the owner of the local feed store – often drop by unannounced and as if they're family. This Saturday in late October 2009 was no different.

I relaxed in the early morning on my favorite recliner. In our home office, Debbie and Dee Jean hovered near our computer. In the kitchen, Barber prepared his talk, flipping between Bible pages filled with scribbles and notes. He drove six hours from Dallas to be here this morning, and after a while, we gathered in the kitchen, discussed former players and the differences between the league now from when it employed us.

Finally, we stepped outside, climbed into our SUV and drove south toward Beeville. We're probably the only people you'll meet who actually want to go to prison.

Debbie sped down the highway, and I sat in the front seat and listened to Barber. Standing 6-foot-3-inches tall and solid, he looks like he could still run block – even at 51 years old. Dee Jean sat in the back and talked on the cell phone with her daughter.

"That's my favorite man in the world right there," Barber said to Dee Jean while pointing at me. He tapped his right cowboy boot on the floor mat and tugged at his black Under Armor T-Shirt. "Coach was the very first man I felt loved me. He saved my life when I first met him. He taught me to trust in me and in the people around me. After football, I wanted to know my coach was going to be in heaven with me. All I know is we are here, and we're on our way together. Today, when he walks into a prison, he turns that prison upside down. He can say more in two minutes than I can say in two hours. Why? Because of who he is."

The prison's tall fences and rows of razor wire seem intimidating to most, but we're used to it by now. We pulled into the guest parking lot and walked toward the guard station. A uniformed man recognized me at the gate.

"Mr. Phillips, is that you? Good to see you," the guard said.

"Good to be seen," I told him.

The T.D.C. Garza West unit is a maximum security prison that houses some of the most violent criminals: gang members, murderers and rapists. The prison chaplain met us outside the prison fence and escorted us to the first of many checkpoints, an outdoor holding cell. Before you enter, you stand for a few seconds and hold your driver's license up to a video camera while it records your information. The first gate opened and then closed behind us. Then, another gate opened and we walked to the administrative building. Once inside, we saw inmates and family members gathered during visitation in a room to our right, but we kept on down a series of narrow concrete hallways. Heavy doors closed and locked behind us. We passed a prison barber shop, never-ending white concrete walls, more doors and clanging locks. The walls seem to narrow the farther you walk into the prison, but I've never felt any sense of suffocation.

The chaplain, a short, potbellied man who insists on hugs instead of handshakes, led us to a small room where he offered us a seat and bottles of water. He pulled a few from the small refrigerator and we talked about how not long ago, we both would have rather had a beer. On the wall: a painting of a cross bridging a cavern.

Barber and I asked if we could enter the administrative segregation wing where the worst offenders stay. The chaplain obliged. A guard opened a thick steel door and we walked inside where we were instantly bordered to our left and right by small, depressing cells. We walked down the hallway slowly. Each man in this lonely hallway, which stretches for 75 feet, hung his head low or covered it with a forest-green blanket. Despair seems to hang in the air here, and it hits you like a fist to the gut. I knocked on a narrow window. A balding, sullen-faced man sat up on his cot and came alive.

"Bum Phillips from the Houston Oilers?" the 45-year-old said.

"Yeah," I told him. "How you doing? Just here to say we love you and we're praying for you. You're in the cell by yourself, but you're never alone. You have to look ahead. You can't look backwards."

I continued to walk from cell to cell, stopping to visit with inmates of all types. They love to talk about the Houston Oilers, Luv Ya Blue or my son and the Dallas Cowboys.

"I'll be," one inmate said, laughing. "I saw you on TV all the time. *We're going to blitz. Every time, we're going to blitz!*"

By now, you might ask: Why do we work with criminals? If you've never been in a prison or visited with an inmate who is locked behind bars, I understand you might not fully appreciate this part. Most of these inmates, though, are just regular people who did something irregular. I used to drink and drive. I could be in prison instead of them – and I remind them of this. I've always been able to talk to people and convince them of what I was thinking. The same is true, I hope, of inmates. They listen.

"Dad has the rare quality of being able to relate to people, whether he's coaching, being a dad or just a regular person," Wade said. "I think that's one of the advantages he's always had."

Maybe we help and maybe we don't. I'm certain if we all had a better belief in the Bible, we'd have fewer criminals. One thing I've come to realize is 99 percent of inmates lacked mentors. They could have been talked out of the trouble they got into.

After a short while, Debbie and Dee Jean walked into the solitary unit to join us. The guards made the women wear bulletproof vests, and I could tell Dee Jean was a bit nervous. She'd never been inside a men's prison.

I continued walking from cell to cell, each of which has white-washed walls, a cot, stainless steel sink, toilet, small table and nothing else.

Barber, busy on the other side of the hallway, pushed his thick fingers between the steel grate and the glass, and asked an inmate to touch his hand. He talked to a young Hispanic inmate who had tattoos on his arm, including an image of Santa Muerta, the Matron Saint of Death. Mexican drug cartels worship the idol and so do many Texas prison gangs. Barber held his Bible and turned to page 771.

"If you accept Jesus, you'll change to represent what God wants," Barber told the inmate, staring him dead in the eyes. "You'll get rid of those gang symbols."

"Yes, sir," the inmate said.

"It's 12:35 p.m. on Oct. 24, 2009," Barber said. "Now, look up to the ceiling for three seconds. OK. Jesus just took your picture. He doesn't use Kodak film. He uses Holy Ghost film. This makes you accountable. You can't pretend you don't know now."

Later, the inmate discussed his visit with Barber.

"I liked it," he said, admitting he's a member of the Texas Syndicate, a notorious and brutal Texas prison gang. "It's surreal, an eye opener. I'm not used to speaking to good people."

Since our first visit to Beeville, Barber and I have toured prisons all over the place. Inmates in the Eastham Unit in faraway Crocket make saddles for the Texas Rangers, and Barber enticed them to make one for Debbie and me, too. In Louisiana at Angola, we coached an intra-prison football game.

"Coach, for a little while I felt like I wasn't in prison," one inmate said after the game.

We all agree inmates who are guilty of a crime should be locked up. But, boy, that's a tough situation and a miserable life.

After 20 minutes, the prison chaplain led us back through the administrative segregation door, down another hallway and to a holding area that opens to the yard. The holding areas remind me of those decompression chambers you see in movies about people who travel to the ocean floor. Outside, inmates walked freely. We walked about 50 feet and toward a metal building located at the middle of the unit. More than 300 prisoners and two guards waited for us inside.

The building has tall ceilings, a concrete floor and enough Texas heat to bake the paint off a truck. Beatles squirmed on the floor. The inmates wore white.

The United States boasts 5 percent of the world's population but 25 percent of its inmates and, as Barber always says, adds another 1,100 prisoners each week. Our country's incarceration rate seems to only get worse.

The chaplain led us along a narrow alleyway, between the 300 inmates and to the front of the room where five chairs faced the troubled audience. The day before, a small riot broke out in the prison and the chaplain asked the men to not leave the area near their seats. We all sat and Barber grabbed the microphone.

"You all ready for some church?" he yelled.

The inmates cheered, stood and clapped. One man sat by an overhead projector, which cast on the back wall words to hymns. Music played over the sound system.

I studied the inmates. Some wore hardened faces and bushy hair; others had baby faces and shaved heads. A few wore eye patches. Most faces turned from stiff to loose, angst-ridden to cheery, when they sang, "Hail Jesus, You're my Lord. Glory to the Lamb, You take me into the land." Some hollered and whistled; others cried. The music, bolstered by the prison choir in the corner, cut the tension in the room like a referee who finally signals first down.

"I wish my church looked like this," Dee Jean said, smiling.

"To see them have such joy and comfort, it's just an emotional thing," Debbie said. "It's something that can convict your heart."

The chaplain asked everyone to bow their heads and pray. Some raised their hands and squinted hard.

Barber took the stage and introduced us all. He moved comfortably, energetically in front of the men.

"No way in the world without Bum Phillips would I be here today," he said, his booming voice filling the large building. "Give your attention to one of the finest men on the face of the planet, one of the finest coaches of all time – Bum Phillips."

I've stood in stadiums with 60,000 and 70,000 screaming fans, but I get about as much joy listening to 300 inmates cheer with the same passion.

"There are a lot of places I could be today," I told the crowd. "I'm retired and I make good money, but I want to be here with you. Believe me, if you're not saved, you'll be right back here once you get out. You owe it to yourself to listen to Mike Barber and me with an open mind. Then you can decide how you want to lead your life. When I was young, I thought I was going to go to heaven like everyone. Coming to a prison for the first time changed my life. I gave up drinking. It's a problem when a man drinks and wakes up regretting what he's done. You need to look at your own life and decide what you need to give up. Maybe it's friends or drugs. Only you can know. I hope you know this: Believe Jesus Christ is your savior. He is your savior."

Debbie and Dee Jean next stood before the microphone. Each leaned against one side of the wooden lectern and shared impromptu thoughts.

"There's nothing greater in the world than to live for Jesus Christ," Debbie said. "We don't come to prison because we like prison. We come here because we love you. I can look around the room and see the love of Christ. Keep loving Jesus and He'll love you back."

When Barber took the stage, he approached the inmates a little differently than we did.

"I'm a blunt talker, and I'm fired up," he said as he moved from side to side and gestured in sweeping motions with his arms. "It's time to grow up and become a man. Just because you bench press 500 pounds does not make you a man. Get up off your lazy butts. Stop wearing your britches so low and get rid of the tattoos. 'What it is, what it is.' I hate gang talk. Learn how to speak. Stop being stupid."

Barber begins his ministry with harsh words, but he speaks them in a way that always gets a laugh. He then softened his approach and spoke quietly.

"I've had troubles in my life, and I had to get honest with myself," he said. "The difference between you and me is you got caught. When you flee from the presence of God you will be nothing to the things of this world. America is sound asleep. I believe more than ever before it's time for men to stand up. When a man changes his life around, 92 percent of his family will follow. Now, how many of you have children? Stand up."

Most of the few hundred stood.

"Now, stand up if you want your children to go to prison."

None did.

"You've been stuck on stupid," Barber said. "You have to get off stupid and wake up and become a man. Relationships put you in prison. It wasn't the drugs or the booze. I want to talk to you about having a relationship with Jesus. Jesus Christ is my quarterback. He's never thrown an incomplete pass, and all passes are for touchdowns. The Bible has the game plan. True sports fans are loyal. Win or lose, sink or swim, they stay with their team. Well, that's how I am as a fan of Jesus Christ."

After 30 minutes, Barber thanked the inmates for their time, and he blessed them. We all stood amid the cheers, walked along the narrow alleyway and into the yard. We left the prison and ate lunch in a Beeville restaurant.

"Some people have to work on their people skills," Barber said, biting into a cheeseburger. "Coach never had to – especially around the inmates."

We talked about Smiley, a former inmate Debbie and I housed after he was released on parole. The prison review board said he could leave after 20 years, but only if he could find a job on the outside. We gave him one, plus a bed in our guest house.

We discussed John Deltorro, a 65-year-old who Barber and I ministered to inside another prison. Deltorro was locked up from 1994 to 2004 for drug convictions. Once outside, he ministered to inmates in the Victoria County Jail, a massive building about 40 minutes north of my home.

"I worshipped Satan before I met Mr. Phillips and Mr. Barber," Deltorro said. "I was possessed with demon spirits that tried to keep me from God. I give all the credit to Mr. Phillips, Mr. Barber and God. Now, I try to bring others to the Lord and share what He can do for them."

Adversity is often the bridge to salvation, and let me tell you, inmates know adversity like few others. It's when we go through our toughest times we can best honor God. Debbie reminds me it's easier to convince a man in prison he should choose Jesus than it often is to convince somebody who lives in freedom.

"Just being a good person doesn't give you the right to enter heaven," Barber said. "You've got to know Him as Lord and Savior. Bum was a good ol' boy, but he'd never stopped to make Jesus the Lord of his life. Bum finally took the time to know Him, and it has changed his life forever."

BUM LESSON: Learn to say 'no' to your kids.

My family is grateful for what it has received since we began ministering in prisons. Almost all my children have joined us in a visit with inmates. We firmly believe God leads you to where you can be most helpful.

You can be most helpful by disciplining your children. While I don't pretend to be a parenting expert, I do know – having met society's so-called worst – too many adults, when children, lacked a strong role model who could positively shape their lives.

You can argue I missed out on too much time with my children, but you can't say I failed to discipline them. These days, both parents work. We have two generations of children we didn't fully discipline. We give them love, but we're not tough enough. When kids do something wrong, they should be punished. You don't have to hit a child to discipline him. Put him in a corner and make him understand why he's in trouble. I think we forgot that as a society.

Too often we fail to guide kids in the little things in life, and then those little things snowball into big things and even worse – prison sentences.

Start today by teaching your kid the word no. Say, "No, you can't stay out until midnight" or "No, you can't be friends with a troublemaker."

God sets rules big and small, and we need to follow them. Parents must set rules, too. As a parent, knowing when to say "no" might make a world of difference in your child's life.

CHAPTER 13

HIS WAY

"I am the way and the truth and the life. No one comes to the Father except through me." – John 14:6.

I was one of the first church members inside, and I absorbed the early-morning buzz of neighbors gathered for Christ. For years, spiritual drought left me parched in certain ways, and this Sunday morning I was thirsty for God's Word.

Debbie and I greeted friends and watched as churchgoers positioned the last of 100 or so folding chairs, which they'd removed just minutes before from rolling racks stored neatly in a closet. The pastor set out "cowboy" bibles and pamphlets, two of which read, "Know the ropes to becoming a Christian" and "I stopped living life my way and started living life God's way."

The Trailhead Cowboy Church, which the pastor says sends cowboys up God's trail, meets at the Julie Wimberley Homemaking Building on U.S. Highway 183 in Goliad. The Goliad County Fairgrounds serve as the backdrop.

Much like the prison services we attend, our church calls a metal building with high ceilings and a concrete floor home. Our church, though, has an open-faced kitchen on the building's south end and a smiling, black-haired woman who brews hot coffee from an industrial-sized pot. This morning, my daughter Andrea stood in the coffee line, and Kimann and her family settled into their seats.

In 2005, my entire family gathered to pray for a different reason. Chest pain forced me to a hospital where doctors found I had three blocked arteries. I had to stay in a hospital bed for days after the triple bypass surgery. I don't get scared easily and often, but the idea of heart surgery was enough to shake me a bit.

"I woke up one morning when he was in the hospital and had Romans 8:38-39 on my heart," Dee Jean said. "'For I am convinced that neither death nor life, neither angels nor demons ... will be able to separate us from the love of God that is in Christ Jesus our Lord.' God wasn't through with Dad yet."

Heart surgery is something I hope you never face. Luckily, I had the love and support of friends and family, who stayed in the hospital to help me through the ordeal. Giff Nielsen, Dan Pastorini, Debbie, my children, their spouses and children gathered for the first time as a family to pray.

Nielsen first prayed near my bed and then in the waiting room while doctors operated. He delivered a private prayer my family still cherishes. They stood in a circle, focused on God, and asked Him to spare my life.

Their prayers worked. When I was finally able to sit up in the intensive care unit, Wade sat nearby. As exhausted as he was, he never left my side. Dee Jean, who developed a passion for writing after finding Christ, wrote a poem, which she read to me while I recovered.

Comforted
I want you to know how God comforted me this week
I prayed and asked all kinds of things; His strength I continued
to seek

He had all six kids together in a waiting room, not fearful
but confident in Him

Wade, Laurie, Mark and I listening to a prayer lifted up for
you by Kim

Oh, there were so many prayers, no one asking the question
"what if"

Laurie, Andrea, and I huddled in a circle with a prayer
from Giff

God used so many people, in so many ways, His power so
amazing to me

Debbie by your side, day and night, your guardian angel we
all would agree

Scripture revealed to me one morning, that nothing can
separate us from the love of God

His words comforted me again as I looked in the mirror, all
I could do was agree and nod

They say you won't remember some of the things that you
said or did

But when you waved that cute little wave to me, God's love
through you could not be hid

We have all been touched, our lives changed, in a way others
may not understand

A prayer over you in ICU by Susan, Debbie, Kimann and
Mark, I felt Jesus' peace in your hand

A lot of tears but they were tears of joy because you have so
much more to do

To spread the love of Jesus to others, is that what this was
all about? God is funny like that. Who would have
ever knew?

I grabbed the hymn book from the chair and sat in my normal
spot in the front row of the church – on the center aisle and
near the pastor's lectern. I don't know what your church is

like, but our Sunday services are like a community celebration filled with ranchers, kids and friends and an eagerness to learn God's Word in simple terms.

I look forward to going to church on Sundays, given the style Pastor David Parks uses during his sermons. He interprets the Bible's lessons into stories anyone can understand. Plus, he's like the people I grew up around. This morning, like most, he wore Wranglers, a blue button-up shirt, green tie outside the collar, handkerchief-scarf, boots and a black cowboy hat. He sports a bushy-but-trimmed goatee and handlebar mustache. He looks like Wyatt Earp, had the gunman traded his pistol for a Bible.

Parks' belt buckle reads "Trailhead Cowboy Church," and he nodded as he tuned a guitar.

Parks stood up front before his sermon and, with another cowboy, warmed up by playing Western tunes. A third man held his small daughter in his lap and banged away on a drum set. The small cowboy band sang a few tune-up songs, and the children danced. Other adults clapped, smiled or visited with country neighbors they hadn't seen in a week. Gospel songs filled the church with inspirational words and a beat I couldn't help but bob my knee to.

"Get on your knees and pray," the cowboys sang. "How marvelous, how wonderful is my savior's love for me. I took Jesus as my savior. You take Him, too."

I wish I could fully convey the feeling you get on a Sunday morning when the warm sounds of Western gospel hit your chest and fill your mind. It's like waking up in the morning to the aroma of warm bread in the kitchen, listening to the sizzle of salty bacon and envisioning your mother smiling wide in your direction.

The stained concrete floor and eight ceiling fans kept the room cool this hot, muggy, South Texas morning. Much of my family sat with me in the front row. Wade couldn't be there, though. The Dallas Cowboys this day kicked off their 2009 regular season in Tampa Bay, and he worked hundreds of miles away, across the Gulf of Mexico in sunny Florida.

It seemed the heat was unbearable everywhere this year. The summer was the region's driest on record. Rain only fell a few times. The cattle roaming the many pastures appeared too thin, bony and helpless. While they had little grass to eat, hay became difficult to yield and even more expensive to buy. Days before, Debbie hopped on our work-styled golf cart, drove a quarter-mile down our paved driveway and beyond the Debbie Dome – the covered arena we use to train horses and avoid the sun. She steered toward the cattle pens.

"Bring 'em on. Wooo, heeeey," she yelled, blowing into a whistle.

Grit, our border-collie cross, cornered some cows and forced them though a large gate. Debbie squinted at the cloudless blue sky, told me not to say the "R" word and then prayed aloud for rain. Grit hopped onto the work cart, and thunder cracked in the distance.

"Please, Lord, please," Debbie said, peeking hesitantly at the sky.

As God is my witness, those blue skies turned dark later on and dropped bucket loads of water for the first time in months.

Parks knew we all had rain on our minds this morning. The pastor took his spot behind the lectern, which is made from wood and shaped into a cross.

"Isn't it so fun to sing when it's green outside?" he said, smiling to a dozen amens. "Heck, even Bum got green this week."

We all cheered, and I chuckled. A man in the back of the room said a prayer.

"Father, we are thankful," the man said as we bowed our heads. "Last week, we raised our hands and we received rain."

The three ministers up front, energized by the rain and the congregation, broke into more Western gospel. "In His time, in His time, He makes all things beautiful, in His time. In Your time, in Your time, You make all things beautiful in Your time."

My family sang, clapped and smiled. Andrea leaned forward in her seat, looked down the aisle at Kimann's children and lured one of my grandsons back to her chair where she bounced the small boy on her knee.

"When I die, halleluja, bye and bye," the ministers sang. "I'll fly away."

Shelly Parks, the pastor's wife, walked to the front of the room and her husband lowered the microphone to near her chin, which barely peeked over the top of the wooden lectern.

"Howdy," she said. She shared the latest news about our church members, upcoming events and then retook her seat.

Pastor Parks likes to begin church this way. He makes coming on Sunday relaxing, joyous and familial. He continues this style during his sermons.

"Turn to Luke, Chapter 19," the pastor said. "People are 100 percent addicted to sin. You need to change." He stepped to the side of the wooden-cross lectern, put an elbow on top, leaned and crossed his brown cowboy boots. "Be honest. Be sincere," he said. "Jesus Christ wants to spend time with you."

I'm sure a great many people were surprised when I became a spiritual man, but I can't blame them and I'm not embarrassed I did. Being a man means doing what's right, whether or not the decision is popular or understood. I always lived by the Golden Rule. It just turns out God's rules are a bit more encompassing. I don't push religion on anyone, but if I get the chance now I use my time to steer people to Christ. Debbie does, too.

"I was really surprised when Bum got into religion," my sister, Jo Annette, said. "I guess, really, I found out when I happened to go down to visit them and Debbie mentioned something about him going into prisons. I didn't even know he was going to church until about six months ago. It surprised me, but I'm glad. I think the football was just absolutely his whole life. He didn't have any room for anything else."

You might wonder how finding Jesus Christ changed my life. First, Debbie and I sat down with Mike Barber, family and other friends and discussed how to improve different parts of our lives. Jesus began to change our thoughts and behaviors, but we wanted to do our part to honor Him, too. We're still under construction and far from perfect, but as a growing network, we hold each other accountable. I feel secure now, safe I will go to heaven.

"Giving our lives to Jesus has meant a huge change in all our lives. We changed as individuals. We grew," Debbie said. "In the sporting world, Bum was a world-class cusser. So was I. It was not that we consciously decided to stop cussing, but God changed us. He changed us into more gentle people. We don't use curse words like we did, and we don't drink anymore. We don't care if you do. The changes that happened for us are not things we require of anyone else."

The faster you can find Jesus Christ, the better. In the end, I suppose it only matters that you find Him. My relationship with my family has also grown in ways I never knew it could. I'm closer to my children and my grandchildren. Dee Jean, my daughter, notices it a lot these days.

"Communication has definitely never been a strong thing in the Phillips family – until now," Dee Jean said. "Now, we can talk about real things. My kids see he changed and who he is now is not the grandpa from before. Now, they know he knows what's going on in their lives. It has totally changed. We're no longer taking baby steps. Now, I can talk to him about anything."

Wade and his wife Laurie visited us not long before the 2010 NFL Draft. Wade joined me in church.

"The message was there, and Pastor Parks did a great job," Wade said. "It was really important to Dad that I came with him, and I think it was great."

I really enjoyed having Wade with me in church. Because of God, I'm closer to my children in ways I just wasn't before. God made Debbie and I more forgiving, and He freed us from a whole lot of stuff you just can't be free of without Christ in your life. Debbie always says I survived World War II because God had bigger plans for me in store. Well, I might just have one more trick up my sleeve.

BUM LESSON: Spend quality time with your family.

Take it from me: When you look back on life you'll wish you spent more time with your family.

When I think back to my NFL career, many of the lasting memories include moments I shared with loved ones.

When Andrea was young, she ate birthday cake with me, Bob Hope and his wife inside the Hopes' hotel room. We didn't have utensils and I still remember Andrea tearing into the cake with her fingers.

Debbie and I invited Kimann and her husband to join us for a Houston Texans game in 2009. On the way home, we listened to the Dallas Cowboys-Denver Broncos game on the radio and cheered for Wade. We stopped in Needville to eat supper at Dee Jean's home. We grabbed sausages out of a bucket, dipped our bread in smoked beans and bacon and washed it down with iced tea.

The Bible discusses the importance of family life and urges parents to convey to children the importance of spirituality.

Spending quality time with your family is a great start.

CHAPTER 14

THE FAMILY WAY

"I will praise you, O Lord, with all my heart; I will tell of all your wonders." – Psalm 9:1

I pushed back from the kitchen table, said goodbye to a neighbor friend and reached for my cowboy hat. Debbie and I were ready to leave our 250-acre ranch for a day trip north and a chance to scout talent at Wade's training camp. We climbed into our SUV and started the engine.

You might say the final chapter of my life is all about a return of sorts – a return to my rural roots, a restoration of meaningful relationships with my children and reflection on my life.

This day, almost three decades after coaching the Houston Oilers and New Orleans Saints, I was primed to return to the sidelines I used to prowl. Debbie and I traveled to a 2009 Dallas Cowboys training camp practice held at the Alamodome in San Antonio. Soon, we'd visit with Wade, Tony Romo and the hordes of media there to catch a glimpse of this year's team. Wade was in his third year as coach, and he'd shaped the team into contenders.

Debbie drove down our paved driveway, and I thought about football. Training camp is a great time to review the players' talents, and I wanted to look at which rookies were good and which were bad. I don't try to influence Wade, although I might make a mention of some things a time or two. As we cruised along, I stared out my passenger window.

I have six children, 23 grandchildren and four great-grandchildren. I missed out on something during all those hours required of coaches. I make up for lost time now, though. I offer my ranch as a place in which we can all regularly gather.

Just days before, Debbie and I hopped onto one of our workhorse golf carts and visited a beautiful nook on our ranch's northwest corner. The land here slopes to the north, and a beautiful vista opens the view to miles of untouched scenery. Dee Jean, my middle child, drove another golf cart, and once we reached the nook, she walked the ground and pointed in excitement to where she and her husband will retire. The future home's windows will capture the views, which will in turn entice their kids to visit often.

"Oh, Dad still loves football, but *it* is not his love," Dee Jean said. "His love is Jesus Christ, and through Him we now have a relationship we never had before. I was just thinking how wonderful it really is since things have changed, getting to come down here and have all those talks. Now, we have good and bad times, tears and laughter."

Dee Jean isn't the only of my children who will call my ranch home. One day not long ago, Kimann's husband Mark and I worked the north area of my ranch. I still move well for a man who took his first steps almost nine decades ago, and I'm as good on a bulldozer as I ever was. I cleared some brush, leveled the ground with my front-end loader, and Mark plucked stumps and limbs from the freshly turned soil. He threw the limbs into the bucket, and I transplanted them into a nearby burn pile. Mark and Kimann moved to Goliad about a year ago. In early 2010, they broke ground on a home that sits less than a football field from my own. I can already look outside to their wraparound porches and see family enjoying the ground Debbie and I hold so dear.

Mark and Kimann are special people and in 2005 built a home of a different sort. They founded Heart Sign, a nonprofit agency that helps deaf children and families by providing classes, workshops and retreats. Not coincidentally, Heart Sign brings families together. Children are entertained in a camp-like setting with counselors who use American Sign Language; other counselors teach parents the language for use in more complicated matters such as parenting and Bible study. We discussed using part of our ranch for a future camp. My folksy colloquialisms might not translate into sign language, but one day my family's hospitality might.

Mark's mother was deaf, and so my son-in-law knows firsthand the struggles of communicating between family members. During the 1950s, his mother's parents didn't sign. Sadly, almost 90 percent of parents with deaf children never learn enough sign language to adequately communicate with their children. Those parents must rely on interpreters for the most important conversations. The way we see it, we ought to help people who need it, and we all agree deaf children need a voice. If you want to learn more about the nonprofit, visit www.HeartSign.org.

"Whenever Bum has seen a need he has tried to help," Debbie said. "I think that's why the people of Houston came to love him and his players so much. You don't see a lot of memorabilia around our house because we've given it away to charity over the years."

As Debbie and I continued toward San Antonio, I thought about the life I've led and the people I've been lucky to meet.

Muhammad Ali visited our training camp when I coached with the Saints; the late President Richard Nixon mailed me a handwritten letter after the Oilers fired me; Johnny Carson interviewed me on "The Tonight Show."

I don't have the energy I once had, and I don't travel as far and often as I'd like to. I often reminisce about players, though, football games and riding horses. Luckily, the phone and doorbell constantly ring. On a recent Friday night, when Debbie and I canceled plans to visit the local ranch rodeo on account of a downpour, Kimann brought five of her six children to the house. Little kids streamed into the living room, through the kitchen and back again. Debbie made chicken salad sandwiches, and the kids gobbled cupcakes, each of which had plastic footballs on top.

As I reminisced, Debbie steered along a narrow farm-to-market road and beyond historic places. Goliad County is a lot like Orange County where I grew up. Texas formed in unique ways in both places. I stared out the passenger window. A post office once stood here; a mansion burned down over there. The Karankawa Indians, a tribe indigenous to the area, once ate captured rivals not far from here. You could invite them over for dinner, but you were it.

My football tribe also made history. Wes Phillips, Wade's son, is a Dallas assistant coach. The three of us are thought to be the first three-generation family to coach in the NFL. In just a few hours, we'd stand together for a rare visit with all of us on a professional football field at the same time.

We drove to the Alamodome and steered into the stadium's underbelly. The Cowboys' team buses, which were also parked under the stadium, idled. We walked between two of them, visited with stadium staff and football folks we've bumped into for years. Security guards called for a driver, who then chauffeured Debbie and me down a long tunnel and onto the spongy turf field.

When we reached the field, we immediately saw Wade, who stood near the 50-yard line and visited with other coaches. The players had yet to take the empty field, and he spotted us right away. Wade jogged to us, hugged us both and visited for about five minutes. We talked about family, how the team looked and plans to gather for the weekend.

During Wade's first Dallas Cowboys news conference, after Jerry Jones hired him in 2007, he talked about cultivating a family environment based on trust, loyalty and common purpose – the same intangibles I hope I instilled in my former teams. I'm proud of Wade. As a head coach, he took three teams to the NFL playoffs, and not many coaches can say the same. In early 2010, he won his first playoff game. Dallas easily defeated rival Philadelphia.

"One thing you'll learn about my family," Wade said, "is the door's always open. Nobody's a stranger. Dad taught us that. I treasure the 10 years I had coaching with Dad more than anything. It was great to be with your hero, your dad and the best coach you've ever been around. As a parent, he changed when the times changed. That's the great thing about him. Once it was OK to tell your kids you love them – which wasn't long ago – he was into that."

Wade jogged back to the middle of the field, and the first of 90 or so players joined him. Debbie and I hopped onto the golf cart, drove around the endzone and toward the 50-yard line. We wanted a spot on the sideline where we could see everything.

When Tony Romo emerged from the tunnel, 13,000 fans screamed. The quarterback veered to his right and jogged the perimeter of the field. Then, he suddenly stopped.

"Hey, Coach," Romo said to me. "It's good to see you. Things are really coming together. Mini camp this year was really important. It's paying dividends in training camp."

I have a lot of respect for Wade and the team's quarterback.

When I coached, a 270-pound man was a big guy. The size of the players nowadays makes those guys look small. There ain't no sissy to quarterbacks of today. I wish they'd put more NFL Films microphones on quarterbacks so people could listen to the hits they take.

Second, when Romo isn't taking hits on the field, he and Wade field a barrage of questions off the field. We all know this is par for the course, but the media attention in Dallas is different than it is elsewhere. Most every decision and every loss makes national headlines. I'm proud of the way they both handle this level of pressure.

Once the players warmed up, Debbie and I moved our golf cart farther away from the sideline. Wherever we moved, so, too, did the cameras and reporters. Debbie parked near the 20-yard line and just feet from where the big offensive linemen performed drills.

"Once Bum rolled in here, everyone took notice," said Mickey Spagnola, a longtime DallasCowboys.com beat writer. "I think it says a lot about him. I think it's just his personality, the homegrown sayings, the way he did things. People felt he was one of their own."

Brady Tinker, an anchorman and reporter for Fox Sports Southwest, said, "Bum's a Texas legend."

After doing a few media interviews, I grabbed a roster, poked my cowboy hat between defensive starters Terence Newman and Ken Hamlin, who were on the sideline for a breather, and studied the rookies. I scanned for players on the edge, those sleepers who might get overlooked. Tight end Jason Witten caught a Romo pass during an offensive drill, and his momentum carried him out of bounds. Players, onlookers and Cowboys staffers – everyone but me – scurried backward.

"Ain't nobody going to run into me," I yelled, laughing. Debbie shot me a look.

The afternoon practice lasted about three hours. Afterward, Wade and Wes joined Debbie and I for a goodbye.

Wes is 31, soft-spoken and calm. He showed Debbie how he coaches blocking. We all agreed we'd gather as a family for the weekend. We decided quickly we'd eat barbecue. There was no sense in arguing considering me, Wade and Wes were all together in one spot. If we wanted to argue, you'd get three opinions: the old school opinion, the middle aged opinion and the youngster's opinion. No decision would ever get made.

After several hugs, we climbed again onto our golf cart, drove across the field and into the tunnel. Wade joined reporters for a press conference.

"I thought we had a good practice," he said. "My dad was there, and he noticed a lot of things. He noticed the players who were *not* in there were really concentrating, which is a good sign."

Later during the regular season, my family drove to Dallas on my 86th birthday so we could watch the first "Monday Night Football" game in the new Cowboys Stadium. We watched the game – I rarely took my eyes off the 60-yard-long video board that hangs from the stadium's rafters – and gathered afterward. Dee Jean and Andrea joked and showered Wade with praise. I reviewed the game statistics with my son and searched for patterns he could use in the following week's game plan. What a birthday gift.

The icing on top of the cake? The Cowboys won.

During the return trip to Goliad – after leaving Wade's training camp practice – Debbie and I talked about the fans, the media and where we might go from here.

First off, we love the fans. They've been so good to us. Having fans is like living in a giant small town. Although I'm not as impressed with myself as others seem to be, I still enjoy it when folks stop and say hi.

Because of the support we've received from others, we remain devoted to charity. We vow to grow Heart Sign, to help Mike Barber with his prison ministry and to help other coaches and families avoid some of the mistakes I made during my time in the demanding profession. We help with Coaches Outreach, a group that seeks to build coaches of conviction through Bible study and marriage retreats. Coaches Outreach encourages and equips coaches and spouses to maintain Christ-like character by using Biblical truths. If you let it, coaching can hurt families. We want coaches to have strong families.

If you boil my ambitions today into one pot, you get something very simple. I want to help in the one way I never did as a coach. I want to teach and spread the Word of God. I know firsthand being a good person is not enough.

We hope this book prompts people to pick up another one – the Bible. All I ask is you give it a chance. If you never check it out, how can you make an educated decision? You might feel you're getting along fine right now, and believe me I once did, too. Your life changes for the better, however – and in ways you never knew possible – once you give your life to Christ.

Maybe He still has something for me to do. I'd still like to help a lot of people – to help our youth find strong mentors. I want to leave this place better than I found it.

Home now from our trip to San Antonio, I looked in appreciation at our beloved ranch. Lord knows He blessed me with an amazing, interesting and rewarding life. I never did win a Super Bowl – didn't get to leave the coaching profession on the highest of notes. But I can't think of a better way to ride off into the sunset than by living my final years as a cowboy and Christian.

I thought for a moment about this book. I peeled back the reasons why I shared certain stories. If you read between the lines, this book really isn't about me. It's about you, the crossroads you face in life and the choices you now have before you. All I did – with the greatest of hopes – was to feed you some food for thought. While my experiences might differ from yours, life has a way of presenting the same scenarios, even if it alters the backdrop. We are, in that sense, the same.

Debbie walked into the living room, stood straight and shared a parting thought with a visitor.

"Bum lived a good life," she said. "If there's a message in all this, it's that good people need Jesus, too."

BUM'S LESSON: Plant the seed.

I hope you've learned something about me, my family and the choices you should consider as you navigate your life. Take it from this weathered cowboy: Mistakes are part of the journey. Just try to avoid taking the same wrong turns twice.

With that in mind, I ask you to plant seeds of faith in your life. If you are a faithful Christian, then please plant the seeds of faith in someone else. You do this in the little things you do – in your words and actions. My family uses poems, conversations and charitable work.

Family members are sometimes the toughest group with which to share Christ, but you can still sneak His message in there. If you don't feel comfortable discussing the subject, give them this book. I'm happy to do the talking for you.

May God bless you and yours.

BIBLIOGRAPHY

CHAPTER ONE: THE HARD WAY

1 : The County Record and The Penny Record: The Community Newspapers of Orange County, Texas; Sept. 5 and Sept 26, 2007.

2: Orange County Texas Historical Society and Howard C. Williams.

3: Texas Escapes Online Magazine: Travel and History; TexasEscapes.com/TexasGulfCoastTowns/OrangeTexas.htm.

4: The Handbook of Texas Online, Texas State Historical Association; Gulf Coast Lumberman, July 1, 1917. Howard C. Williams, ed., Gateway to Texas: The History of Orange and Orange County (2d ed., Orange, Texas: Heritage House Museum, 1988).

5: He Ain't No Bum, Bum Phillips and Ray Buck (A Signet Book: New American Literary, 1979), 18.

CHAPTER TWO: THE HARDER WAY

1: Tom's Inflation Calculator, Tom Halfhill, Halfill.com/Inflation.

2: The Prize, Daniel Yergin, (New York: Simon & Schuster, 1991), 69; Wikipedia.

3: The Handbook of Texas Online, Texas State Historical Association; John M. Duncan, An Eye-Opener: The Standard Oil-Magnolia Compromise: The Whole Cold Truth (San Antonio, 1915). History of Petroleum Engineering (Dallas: American Petroleum Institute, 1961).

4: The Handbook of Texas Online, Texas State Historical Association; J. Evetts Haley, Charles Goodnight (Norman: University of Oklahoma Press, 1949). C. Robert Haywood, Trails South: The Wagon-Road Economy in the Dodge City-Panhandle Region (Norman: University of Oklahoma Press, 1986). J. Marvin Hunter, Trail Drivers of Texas (2 vols., San Antonio: Jackson Printing, 1920, 1923; 4th ed., Austin: University of Texas Press, 1985).

5: University of Arkansas Razorback Basketball, (Arkansas Razorbacks Athletics Department Media Guide, 2008-2009), 167.

CHAPTER THREE: WAY TOO LONG

1: United States Marine Corps Air Stations of World War II, M.L. Shettle, Jr., (Schaertel Publishing Co., 2001), 84; Wikepedia.

2: U.S.S. LST 494 Association website, lst494.freeyellow.com/LST_494_ Higgins_Boat_LCVP_.html

3. He Ain't No Bum, Bum Phillips and Ray Buck (A Signet Book: New American Literary, 1979), 29.

4. Historical accounts provided by Dan Marsh's United States Marine Corps Raiders with permission of Louis Marsh.

CHAPTER FIVE: THE WORKMAN'S WAY

1: Pigskin Pulpit: A Social History of Texas High School Football Coaches, Ty Cashion (Texas State Historical Association, 1998), 13-15.

2: Pigskin Pulpit: A Social History of Texas High School Football Coaches, Ty Cashion (Texas State Historical Association, 1998), 1; 14-15.

3: Pigskin Pulpit: A Social History of Texas High School Football Coaches, Ty Cashion (Texas State Historical Association, 1998), 203.

4: Pigskin Pulpit: A Social History of Texas High School Football Coaches, Ty Cashion (Texas State Historical Association, 1998), x; Foreword by O.A. "Bum" Phillips.

CHAPTER SIX: THE COLLEGE WAY

1: He Ain't No Bum, Bum Phillips and Ray Buck (A Signet Book: New American Literary, 1979), 1-2; Foreword by Paul "Bear" Bryant.

CHAPTER NINE: A FOOTBALL FAMILY'S WAY

1. He Ain't No Bum, Bum Phillips and Ray Buck (A Signet Book: New American Literary, 1979), 235

AUTHOR BIO

GABE SEMENZA, a native of Helena, Montana, is an award-winning writer and editor. He has won countless Texas and national awards for investigative and narrative journalism. In 2010, he was named Star Reporter of the Year for all newspaper categories by the Texas Associated Press Managing Editors Association. The same year, he also won national awards for a series about human and drug smuggling along the U.S.-Mexico border, as well as a Society of Professional Journalists Sigma Delta Chi Award for his series about federal stimulus spending. He lives in South Texas with his pregnant wife and three dogs.